What people are saying about …

The 30-Day Praise Challenge for Parents

"Let's face it—our kids disappoint us and sometimes make wrong choices that create disagreement in our marriages. We know we need to pray for our children, but how? Becky Harling has written a book that reveals how to use praise as a transformational tool for moving from worry to hope-filled peace based on God's truth. This book will not only help you to be a better parent, but it will make your marriage stronger too. We highly recommend it!"

Gene and Carol Kent, of Speak Up Ministries

"Praise God for Becky Harling! This 30-day challenge is a gift to modern parents everywhere! For many, raising kids in the twenty-first century generates anxiety, fear, and regret. What parent doesn't feel tired, frazzled, or inadequate at times? But Becky provides a pathway to peace—praising God for your child's unique design and entrusting care to their heavenly Father. Mom or Dad, if you're ready to move beyond the busyness and comparison traps in our culture, get this book. As you draw closer to Christ, you'll discover a newfound confidence and freedom in raising your kids!"

Tim Lucas, lead pastor of Liquid Church

"I love any challenge that makes me a better person, but Becky Harling has created one to make me a better parent. I have never seen such a positive, proactive, and praise-centered parenting partnership with God. Start the 30-day challenge! I am ready to be a happier mother and enjoy my kids (and grandkids) more!"

Pam Farrel, bestselling coauthor of *Men Are Like Waffles, Women Are Like Spaghetti* and *The 10 Best Decisions Every Parent Can Make*

"Where was this book when I was raising my children? I read so many parenting books, but this is the one I needed! Take the 30-day challenge. You will be changed and so will your children!"

Linda Dillow, author of *What's It Like to Be Married to Me?* and *Calm My Anxious Heart*

"Get ready to exchange your anxiousness for rest. As you participate in *The 30-Day Praise Challenge for Parents*, you'll experience the powerful presence of God in a fresh way. It will change your home forever when, as a parent, you learn to praise God."

Arlene Pellicane, author of *31 Days to Becoming a Happy Wife*

"Praise God for the privilege of the wild ride of parenting! And praise God through the wild ride of parenting. If you're wondering how to keep the praise going (even when someone put army men in the toaster while someone else buttered the cat), Becky Harling's book *The 30-Day Praise Challenge For Parents* is just the praise ticket for the ride! Gotta love what a praise focus does. More praise, less stress—just what we need to experience that 'throw your hands in the air' kind of joy all along the way!"

Rhonda Rhea, TV host, author of twelve books, including *Espresso Your Faith*

"If you are a parent, please get this book and set it on your nightstand. You will want to read and refer to it again and again. Parenting is a journey that takes us to the highest of mountains but also through the deepest valleys. While every parent must learn about child development and seek to implement wise parenting strategies, there will be times when it feels as though you can do nothing but sink to your knees. Thankfully, that is one of our strongest positions as a parent, and this book provides both spiritual and practical support to parents throughout the developmental stages of their children from infancy through launching into adulthood. Whether your child is soaring or sinking, thriving or struggling, this book will help you use the secret weapon of praise to gain perspective, courage, insight, and strength as you seek to train your children in the way they should go."

Sue Badeau, adoptive parent, national speaker, and author of *Are We There Yet?*

"*The 30-Day Praise Challenge for Parents* is a needed weapon in the hands of every praying mom and dad. Praise is a powerful foundation on which families can grow in their relationship with God and each other."

Saundra Dalton-Smith, author of *Come Empty*

the **30** day
praise
challenge
for parents

the 30day praise challenge

for parents

becky harling

David C Cook

transforming lives together

THE 30-DAY PRAISE CHALLENGE FOR PARENTS
Published by David C Cook
4050 Lee Vance View
Colorado Springs, CO 80918 U.S.A.

David C Cook Distribution Canada
55 Woodslee Avenue, Paris, Ontario, Canada N3L 3E5

David C Cook U.K., Kingsway Communications
Eastbourne, East Sussex BN23 6NT, England

The graphic circle C logo is a registered trademark of David C Cook.

The website addresses recommended throughout this book are offered as a
resource to you. These websites are not intended in any way to be or imply an
endorsement on the part of David C Cook, nor do we vouch for their content.

Unless otherwise noted, all Scripture quotations are taken from the Holy
Bible, New International Version˚, NIV˚. Copyright © 1973, 1984 by Biblica,
Inc.™ Used by permission of Zondervan. All rights reserved worldwide. www.
zondervan.com. Scripture quotations marked NLV are taken from the New Life
Version Bible, copyright © 1969 by Christian Literature International. Used
by permission. All rights reserved; ESV are taken from The Holy Bible, English
Standard Version˚ (ESV˚), copyright © 2001 by Crossway, a publishing ministry
of Good News Publishers. Used by permission. All rights reserved; PH are taken
from J. B. Phillips: *The New Testament in Modern English*, revised editions © J. B.
Phillips, 1958, 1960, 1972, permission of Macmillan Publishing Co. and Collins
Publishers; NLT are taken from the *Holy Bible*, New Living Translation, copyright
© 1996, 2007 by Tyndale House Foundation. Used by permission of Tyndale
House Publishers, Inc., Carol Stream, Illinois 60188. All rights reserved; and KJV
are taken from the King James Version of the Bible. (Public Domain.) Scripture
quotations marked NKJV are taken from the New King James Version˚. Copyright
© 1982 by Thomas Nelson, Inc. Used by permission. All rights reserved.
The author has added italics to Scripture quotations for emphasis.

LCCN 2014940403
ISBN 978-1-4347-0578-5
eISBN 978-0-7814-1239-1

© 2014 Becky Harling

The Team: John Blase, Liz Heaney, Amy Konyndyk, Nick
Lee, Jack Campbell, Helen Macdonald, Karen Athen
Cover Design: Amy Konyndyk
Cover Photo: iStockphoto

Printed in the United States of America
First Edition 2014

1 2 3 4 5 6 7 8 9 10

063014

To my four children:
Bethany, Josiah, Stefanie, and Kerith.
Dad and I are so thankful for each
of you, for your walks with God,
for your amazing spouses.
I have had the privilege of watching God do
exceedingly abundantly more than I could
have asked or imagined in each of your lives.
I praise God continually for each of you!

contents

Part One

the challenge

why parents should
give praise a chance

Parenting can be simultaneously wonderful and difficult. I know because I've been there. I have raised four kids and now have five grandchildren. While I have loved most of my moments as a parent, there have been days when I wondered if I would lose my mind or, worse, if I would mess up their minds. I wanted to parent well, but I struggled with anxiety. At times all I could do was cry out to God, "Help! I have no idea what to do!"

Well into my parenting journey, I began a new spiritual practice that not only enhanced my relationship with God, but it also made me a better parent and strengthened my relationships with my children. The practice began with breast cancer. If anything throws an unexpected curveball at your parenting style, it's cancer!

With the diagnosis of cancer, my anxiety went off the charts. I wondered, *Will I even be alive to finish raising my kids? Will they feel so angry with God for allowing me to get cancer that they will walk away from their faith? If I die, how will Steve cope with being a single dad?* Never had I felt such a desperate need for God. I called a friend and asked her to pray with me.

After we prayed, my friend did something I did not see coming. She challenged me to spend twenty minutes a day for the next week in pure praise. I remember thinking, *What a crazy idea! Wouldn't that be hypocritical? I don't exactly feel thankful for cancer, and I hardly feel like shouting, "Hallelujah, I'm facing a double mastectomy!"* But after wrestling with the idea, I decided to give praise a shot. After all, what did I have to lose?

What I experienced in those five days radically changed my life. I struggled less with anxiety and felt more peace than I ever had before. I experienced the presence of God in new and dynamic ways that left me hungry for more. By the end of the week, I was hooked. **I learned that praising God isn't just some glib hallelujah when finances are prospering,**

your health is flourishing, and your family is thriving. Praising God is an intentional declaration by faith that exalts God above your life circumstances.

As I continued in my journey of praise, I began to exalt God for His sovereign control in the lives of my children. I thanked Him by faith that even if He took my life, He would care for my children. I praised Him that just as He was calming my fears, He would calm the fears of my kids. Gradually, I noticed that praise was quieting my anxiety, and it was providing a protective shield over my family.

As I praised God intentionally, my children's faith began to grow deeper and Satan's tactics to destroy our family were defeated. Spiritual victories were won in our family, and relationships grew stronger. As I exalted God for what He was doing in each child's life, my need to nag my kids diminished—and guess what? My relationship with each child improved! As I have continued this practice through the years, I have come to believe that praising God is a powerful tool for building strong families.

Friend, Satan, the enemy of your soul, wants to kill, steal, and destroy your family. But when you praise God, Satan flees! This is especially true when you combine praise with

Scripture. When you declare God's glorious faithfulness over your children, you provide a protective covering over your home, and in the process, you are transformed.

I am guessing you picked up this book because you want to be the best parent possible. Perhaps you are looking for a way to spend time with God that feels doable in the craziness of raising kids. Perhaps you feel discouraged with where your children are spiritually and are looking for a way to strengthen your hope. No matter why you picked up this book, I promise you that if you take this challenge, your life will change! Here's the challenge:

Spend twenty minutes a day for thirty consecutive days intentionally praising God for His work in your child's life.

In part 2, "30 Days of Praise," you'll find thirty days of praise challenges built on different aspects of parenting. The majority of the first fifteen days focus on you as a parent, and the majority of the last fifteen days focus on your child. Each day begins with a Scripture-based invitation to praise God for some aspect of His character. Written as from God Himself, these invitations are designed to help you hear God's voice. These invitations are not the inspired Word of God, but they are based on Scripture and represent what I believe God would say to parents. Praise was His idea in the first place. He invites us to praise Him, not because He is insecure or egotistical, but because He knows that as we worship Him, we become more like Him. Each day also includes guidance for how to praise God, suggestions for music that can enhance your worship, and a journal idea to help you process your praise journey and the changes you are experiencing.

In addition, each day includes a prayer of praise. We worship a triune God, so the prayers are directed to one or more members of the Trinity: God the Father; God the Son, Jesus Christ; and God the Holy Spirit. As you intentionally praise each member of the triune God, your relationship with each will grow.

Part 3, "Taking It Further," contains additional ideas and tips to enhance your praise journey, including how to praise God when you and your spouse don't agree on parenting issues and when your child is adopted or has been affected by divorce. To get the most out of your praise journey, you will need:

Intentionality. The season of raising children is one of the busiest you will face in life. You will need to make an intentional choice to create the space to do this challenge.

Praise is not a legalistic practice; so if you miss a day, don't worry or feel guilty. Just pick up where you left off. Decide that you are going to create the space to do the challenge. Perhaps the best time for you is early in the morning before your family gets up. Or it might be during your children's nap time or in the evening after everyone is tucked in bed or on your lunch break. Be creative. You might do your twenty minutes of praise while running, driving, or taking a shower. The great thing about praising God is that you can do it anywhere! So ask Him to help you find the time to do the challenge. I'm guessing He'll answer in ways you have not expected.

Praise music. On page 223 is a list of praise songs that I encourage you to listen to during this challenge. If you download the songs ahead of time, your praise time will be uninterrupted. However, if you prefer, you can listen to the songs by accessing the YouTube or Spotify playlists that are on my website: www.beckyharling.com. If you find that the songs I've chosen don't appeal to you, that's fine. Just find praise music that helps you focus on the presence of God.

Perseverance. You may be tempted to quit, especially if you don't see immediate results. Please don't stop. God honors faithfulness. If you have a tough day with your kids, I'm betting that Satan is going to whisper his "blah, blah, blah" in your ear, trying to convince you that praising God makes no difference. Don't listen to him! He's a liar from way back (John 8:44). Listen to the voice of God gently inviting you to come and praise Him. It takes discipline to persevere in praise, but I promise you, if you do, you'll be blessed!

To make it personal. I encourage you to make the prayers personal by replacing references to "your child" with the name(s) of your child(ren) and by filling in the blanks in the prayers. Do this in a way that feels meaningful to you. You may notice that on some days I use *him* when referring to your child and on others I use *her*. Please feel free to use the pronoun that applies to your child(ren).

A journal. At the end of each day, I've included a question for you to write a response to in a journal. There are no right or wrong answers to these questions. The purpose is to help you process and record the changes you are experiencing.

Some of the questions ask you to imagine or envision the positive changes you would like to see and experience. I believe that God uses our imaginations to help us dream and experience His presence. Dreaming helps sustain our hope. So don't be afraid of dreaming and imagining what God might do in your life and in the life of your child.

A Bible. Even though most of the scriptures are written out for you, use and become familiar with your Bible as you do this practice. Underline and date the verses that apply to your prayers of praise for your child. You can even praise God in advance for what He is going to do in your child's heart. I have done this, and now as I go back through my Bible, I am encouraged and strengthened by how many times God answered the cries of my heart. Feel free to underline, highlight, and date your Bible. It will be such an encouragement to you in years to come.

If you take this challenge, you will change, and you will see changes in your children and in your family life. The power of praising God is remarkable! Let's get started.

Part Two

30 days of praise

Day 1

For you created my inmost being;
you knit me together in my mother's womb.
I praise you
because I am fearfully and wonderfully made.

Psalm 139:13–14

The Invitation

Beloved, before I set the earth into motion, I knew I would design your child to reflect My image. I considered every intricate detail of his unique design. I imagined his personality and his specific physical characteristics. As I knit your baby together, I crafted every brain cell, chose the color of his hair, and designed the pigment of his eyes. Praise Me that your child is fearfully and wonderfully made in My image. My design is good! I don't make mistakes. I know that your child may have personality traits that you would like to change. Instead of plotting how to change him or comparing him to other children, why not praise Me for those qualities? My thoughts are infinitely higher than yours. As you praise Me, My Spirit will strengthen your trust in My sovereignty. Watch and see what I will do as you faithfully praise Me for your child's unique design. (Ps. 139:13–14; Gen. 1:27; Gen. 1:31; Isa. 55:8)

> O LORD, you have searched me
>   and you know me.
> You know when I sit and when I rise;
>   you perceive my thoughts from afar.
>   (Ps. 139:1–2)

Parents often compare their child with other children, wishing that their child had stronger skills in some area or another. Today, when you feel tempted to compare or criticize your child, stop and praise God instead for your child's unique design. Dare to thank Him for the very qualities that frustrate you most about your child.

Listen

Listen to "Open Up Our Eyes" by Elevation Worship. As you listen, rededicate yourself as a parent and make a commitment to praise God intentionally over your child. Ask the Holy Spirit to open your eyes to discover new truths about God during this challenge and to discern more wisdom concerning your child. Then listen to "Ascribe" by New Life Worship featuring Cory Asbury, and "Remind Me Who I Am" by Jason Gray, and praise God that He designed your child perfectly and according to His plan.

Pray

Oh, God, I stand in awe of how You masterfully created my child and knit him together in the womb. I praise You for how You wired him intentionally. I praise You for my child's physical, intellectual, emotional, and social design. Even before he was born, You set him apart for Your glory and pleasure. How I praise You that You carefully and skillfully crafted every detail of his body to reflect Your image. Truly, my child is Your artistic masterpiece! You are not disappointed with the way he turned out. You delight in his unique design and call it "good." Holy One, I pray that You would continually open my eyes to how magnificent Your design is. I praise You that You understand not only every thought and feeling in my mind and heart but also all the thoughts and feelings of my child. I praise You that before my child speaks even a word You know and understand his thoughts. I praise You that as I become a student of my child, You will guide me in how to parent him and direct him in the ways he should go. (1 Tim. 4:4; Ps. 139:1–2; Jer. 1:5; Ps. 139:4; Prov. 22:6)

Journal

Spend a few moments today writing down specific qualities that comprise your child's unique design. Write out a prayer of gratitude for your child's specific personality.

Day 2

"Not by might nor by power,
but by my Spirit,"
*says the L*ORD *Almighty.*
Zechariah 4:6

The Invitation

Dear one, I know that you often feel inadequate as a parent. Of all the callings, parenting is one of the most difficult. Whether you have toddlers, tweens, or teens, you'll face unexpected challenges on your parenting journey. I want you to know and trust that My Spirit is the perfect match for your inability. I have called you to parent the specific child I have placed in your care. Though you are not perfect, I will be faithful to help you parent. Praise Me that I promise to equip you moment by moment. As you praise Me, My Spirit will strengthen, guide, and empower you to be the parent I have called you to be. Even when you are unsure of how to pray for your child, My Spirit will show you how to intercede for her. Praise Me that through My Spirit, you can do all things, even parent a challenging child. Rest assured, I've got you covered. My strength is perfected in your weakness. Lean into My strength and praise Me often. (John 16:13; 1 Thess. 5:24; Rom. 8:26; Phil. 4:13; 2 Cor. 12:9)

> I can do everything through him who gives
> me strength. (Phil. 4:13)

Almost every parent I know feels inadequate at some point. God promises to empower parents who look to Him for help and praise Him by faith. Today, when feelings of inadequacy flood your mind, immediately praise God for choosing you to be your child's parent. What God calls you to do, He empowers you to do. Praise Him by faith that His Spirit will fill you with wisdom and direction today as you parent.

Listen

Listen to "Steady My Heart" by Kari Jobe, "I Will Look Up" by Elevation Worship, and "Lord, I Need You" by Chris

Tomlin. As you listen, praise God that He has fully equipped you to parent.

Pray

I praise You, Holy Spirit, that You promise to fill me and empower me to parent. God, sometimes parenting is so hard! But I praise You that when I am weak, You are strong. When I lack wisdom, You give wisdom. When I lack patience, You've got plenty. When I feel like quitting, You empower me to persevere. When it feels like everything is falling apart, You are in control. I am so thankful that Your Spirit indwells me and continually pours new courage and strength into my weary soul. Thank You that You are faithful. Lord, help me not to throw away my confidence but to choose to praise You even in the moments when I feel inadequate. (John 14:17–18; James 1:5; Heb. 10:35–36)

Journal

Read Hebrews 10:35–36. In what ways do you "throw away" your confidence as a parent? For example, if you practice negative self-talk ("I'm the worst mother in the world") or compare yourself to other parents ("My friends all seem to be so patient with their kids. Why do I struggle with impatience?"), you are throwing away your confidence.

Day 3

*The L*ORD *is my light and my salvation—*
whom shall I fear?
*The L*ORD *is the stronghold of my life—*
of whom shall I be afraid?

Psalm 27:1

The Invitation

Fear and anxiety are a part of every parent's journey. News reports filled with stories of violence, crimes against children, accidental tragedies, and changing moral codes stir up parental fear. I understand that you long to safeguard your child; you want to protect his physical and emotional well-being, innocence, and view of the world. But, My child, I don't want you to live in captivity to fear. I long for you to turn your panic into praise. Praise Me that I am your refuge and strength. Praise Me that nothing catches Me by surprise. Praise Me that I will hide your child in the shelter of My holy presence. I am able to protect him beyond your human efforts. Train your mind to trust Me. I always listen to your cries for help. As you faithfully praise Me, I will strengthen your heart to trust Me more. When you are tempted to believe that I don't see what's happening, praise Me that My eye is never off your child for even a moment. Even when your child is the victim of unfortunate circumstances, I am able to bring good out of evil. Nothing can separate your child from My love. (Ps. 46:1–2; Ps. 47:8; Ps. 31:20; Ps. 91:1–2; Ps. 56:3–4; Ps. 31:22; Rom. 8:28, 38–39)

Do not be afraid, for I am with you. (Isa. 43:5)

I believe that praise is a parent's most effective weapon against anxiety. As you practice turning your panic into praise, God will slowly help you experience more peace in your parenting. Today, whenever anxious thoughts besiege your mind, immediately start praising God that He is loving and powerful and better equipped than you to protect your child.

Listen

Listen to "We Won't Be Shaken" by Building 429, "Oceans" by Hillsong United, and "You Make Me Brave" by Bethel Music and Amanda Cook.

Pray

Lord Jesus, I confess that I struggle with anxiety and fear. I long to protect my child from every evil influence, and sometimes my worries consume me. I praise You, Holy One, that You are both sovereign and loving. Power and might are in Your hands, and no one can withstand You. I praise You that I can trust You to protect my child because You love my child even more than I do. I praise You that nothing, absolutely nothing, can separate my child from Your love. Thank You that You haven't given me a spirit of fear; rather, You have called me to courage and a sound mind. As I praise You, I know that You will increase my faith to trust You more. Take me so deeply into the ocean of Your faithfulness that I become the bold and courageous parent You desire me to be. (2 Chron. 20:6; Rom. 8:38–39; 2 Tim. 1:7)

Journal

Make a list of all your fears for your child. Then go back through the list and surrender each fear to the Lord. It can be helpful to create a "worry jar." List each worry on a piece of paper and put it in your worry jar as you surrender it to God. Also make a "praise jar." Every time you put a worry in your worry jar, immediately write down something you can praise God for and put it in your praise jar.

Day 4

By wisdom a house is built,
and through understanding it is established;
through knowledge its rooms are filled
with rare and beautiful treasures.

Proverbs 24:3–4

The Invitation

My beloved, every day you are faced with countless parenting decisions. It's easy to feel confused and overwhelmed by all the opinions and theories about what your child needs. But remember, I am the source of all wisdom. I have created every child to be one of a kind, and that means there is no one "right" method of parenting. If it were that easy, you wouldn't need Me. When you lack wisdom and understanding, come to Me and praise Me as the never-ending source of wisdom. I understand your child better than you do. After all, I created her. Praise Me for My knowledge of your child. If you will only ask, I will give you the wisdom that you need, moment by moment. As you worship Me, I will help you sift through all the information and advice that bombard you every day. Praise Me in advance for the wisdom I will give you today. (Prov. 3:19; Prov. 2:6, 10; Ps. 139:2; James 1:5)

> Trust in the LORD with all your heart and lean not on your own understanding; in all your ways acknowledge him, and he will make your paths straight. (Prov. 3:5–6)

There is no shortage of advice for parents. Often we run to the "experts" for help, rather than running to God as the source of all wisdom. No one understands your child better than He does. Praise Him today that as you ask Him, He will direct you and give you discernment regarding what's best for your child.

Listen

Listen to "Come to Me" by Bethel Music featuring Jenn Johnson, "You Are My Vision" by Rend Collective Experiment, and "Help Me Find It" by Sidewalk Prophets.

Pray

Lord, I worship You as the source of all wisdom. At times I become overwhelmed by all the parenting advice out there. Help me to remember to come to You first. I praise You that Your wisdom is perfect and holy. You've never needed a counselor or advice from anyone. There's never been a problem or dilemma that You couldn't solve. Thank You that You alone know what is best for my child and for our family. I worship and exalt You! Thank You that as I praise You, Your voice will whisper in my ear the way to go. I can count on You to direct my paths and give me understanding. I praise You that You know my child far better than I ever could. I praise You, Lord Jesus, in advance for the wisdom You will give me today. (Prov. 9:10; Isa. 30:21; Rom. 11:33–34; James 1:5)

Journal

In what particular areas of your child's life do you need wisdom? Write about those areas in your journal, and then write a prayer of praise, thanking God by faith that He will give you the wisdom you need.

Day 5

The Invitation

Precious one, I know how awful you feel when you mess up with your child. Whether you lose patience, speak in an angry tone, or fail to show compassion, come to Me as the grace giver. You feel guilty for not measuring up to some unattainable standard. Rather than sinking into shame, praise Me for My grace. There is no punishment or condemnation for those who are in Christ Jesus. Every time you mess up with your child, breathe in My grace and exhale My praise. This trains you to live in My grace and also models a lifestyle of grace for your child. Praise Me because all your mistakes and failures were atoned for by the blood that Jesus

shed on the cross. The more you praise Me for My grace, the more
you will enjoy the freedom of My grace in your home life. (Eph.
2:8; Rom. 8:1; Rom. 3:25; Gal. 5:1)

> It is for freedom that Christ has set us free.
> Stand firm, then, and do not let yourselves
> be burdened again by a yoke of slavery.
> (Gal. 5:1)

No job triggers as much guilt as parenting. But guilt and
shame are not God's will for His children. When guilt threat-
ens to sabotage your peace today, immediately start praising
God for His grace. I believe the more you praise God for His
grace, the more the Holy Spirit will strengthen you to trust
God's grace and the more you will live in freedom.

Listen

Listen to "Your Grace Finds Me" by Matt Redman, "This Is
Amazing Grace" by Phil Wickham, and "Hello, My Name Is"
by Matthew West.

Pray

Lord Jesus, I praise You for Your grace. I fail so often as a parent, whether through my words, thoughts, or actions. Thank You that You stand ready to forgive me. I praise You that when I feel guilty, I can come to You and confess my faults and You immediately offer grace. I am so thankful that You choose to use me in my child's life, even though I make so many mistakes along the way. I praise You that our home can be a place of grace, where those who sin are offered love and forgiveness. Just as You forgive me, let me offer forgiveness to my child. Thank You that You don't demand perfection from me as a parent and that You love me anyway. Oh, Lord, I want to praise You forever for Your grace. Thank You! Remind me today to breathe in Your grace and exhale Your praise. (Ps. 130:4; Eph. 4:32; Ps. 103:3, 14)

Journal

In what areas of parenting do you struggle with guilt? What do you think your guilt feelings stem from?

Day 6

I wait for you, O LORD;
you will answer,
O Lord my God.

Psalm 38:15

The Invitation

I know how excruciating it feels when you are waiting for Me
to act on behalf of your child. You are tempted to get angry with
Me and to doubt that I know what's best. You long for Me to
act quickly, but I am training your child for future use in My
kingdom. I have not forgotten your child, and I am working
behind the scenes to accomplish My purposes in his life. Praise
Me in advance for how I am going to answer your prayers.
Declare by faith that your hope is in Me. As a parent, you are
tempted to take matters into your own hands. Be strong, and
resist the temptation to move ahead of Me. Instead, bow your

timetable before Me. Kneel down, worship Me, and praise Me that I am on time in your child's life. Those who praise Me are strengthened to wait patiently. As you praise Me, My Spirit will pour hope into your soul. (Ps. 39:7; Isa. 40:31; Ps. 95:6–7; Ps. 131:2)

> I wait for the LORD, my soul waits, and in
> his word I put my hope. (Ps. 130:5)

When waiting for God to answer your prayers for your child, instead of giving in to discouragement, praise Him for what He will do. Praise will help keep hope alive as you wait. In your praise time today, focus on these promises for your child:

> Because of the LORD's great love we are not
> consumed, for his compassions never fail.
> They are new every morning; great is your
> faithfulness. I say to myself, "The LORD is
> my portion; therefore I will wait for him."
> (Lam. 3:22–24)

I have swept away your offenses like a cloud, your sins like the morning mist. Return to me, for I have redeemed you. (Isa. 44:22)

I will go before you and will level the mountains; I will break down gates of bronze and cut through bars of iron. I will give you the treasures of darkness, riches stored in secret places, so that you may know that I am the LORD, the God of Israel, who summons you by name. (Isa. 45:2–3)

You will eat the fruit of your labor; blessings and prosperity will be yours. (Ps. 128:2)

Then the Father will give you whatever you ask in my name. (John 15:16)

(For additional promises see "Using Scripture to Praise God for His Work in Your Child's Life" in part 3, "Taking It Further.")

Listen

Listen to "The Lord Our God" by Kristian Stanfill, "I Wait for the Lord" by Jeremy Camp, and "Waiting Here for You" by Christy Nockels.

Pray

Lord God, You are King over all the earth, and Your timing is perfect. You understand how desperately I long for You to answer my prayers for my child. In my humanness I don't always understand Your timing. Your ways are so much higher than my ways, and Your purposes are beyond my understanding. Holy One, I bow before You and worship You as the One who knows what is best for my child. Though I would love to step in and speed things up, I will instead exalt You as the One who is always on time. I acknowledge that often the greater the delay, the deeper the work You are doing in my child's life. I praise You that You invite me to quietly and confidently wait for You to act. (Isa. 55:8; Ps. 95:6; Isa. 48:10; Isa. 30:15)

Journal

In what areas of your child's life are you having difficulty waiting for God to act? How might praising God during your
waiting period quiet your heart?

Day 7

For great is your love,
higher than the heavens;
your faithfulness reaches to the skies.

Psalm 108:4

The Invitation

Rejection in your child's life is inevitable, and yet nothing prepares you for how difficult it will feel. When your child is rejected, it tears your heart in shreds. I understand. I watched My own Son experience rejection and humiliation at the hands of others. Friends, sports teams, and colleges may reject your child, but I never will. Her name is engraved on the palms of My hands. Lift up your eyes, and see how deeply I love your child. When your child experiences rejection, I will comfort her and wipe away her tears. Teach your child to cling to My love. Exalt Me that I am building resiliency into her life. Thank Me that before the foundation of the world I chose your child to be holy and blameless in My sight. Praise Me for My stubborn love of your child. (Isa. 53:3; Isa. 49:16, 13; Ps. 56:8; Eph. 1:4)

> I have loved you with an everlasting love;
> I have drawn you with loving-
> kindness. (Jer. 31:3)

Remind yourself today that God loves your child even more than you do. He sings over her, delights in her, comforts her, and pursues her. When your child experiences rejection, immediately begin praising God that He will never reject her. He loves and cherishes your child completely.

Listen

Listen to "Unfailing Love" by Chris Tomlin, "Your Love Is Like a River" by Third Day, and "One Thing Remains" by Kristian Stanfill on the *Passion: White Flag* album.

Pray

Father, when my child experiences rejection, it kills me. Thank You that You understand my feelings because Your precious Son also experienced rejection, mockery, and betrayal. I exalt You, because nothing can separate my child from Your love, and Your love for her never fails. Thank You that You take great delight in her and even sing over her. Thank You that every time she experiences rejection it gives her the opportunity to sink down deeper into Your love. I praise You that You are able to strengthen her through Your Spirit so that she will be able to comprehend how wide and long and high and deep is the love of Christ. Thank You that You will do more than all I can ask or imagine to bring good out of this difficult season. (Luke 18:32; Rom. 8:36–37; Ps. 36:7; Zeph. 3:17; Eph. 3:18, 20)

Journal

If your child has experienced rejection recently, write a prayer to God expressing your feelings with the most honest language you can muster. Then write a prayer of praise for how God will turn the rejection around for good in your child's life.

Day 8

So do not fear, for I am with you;
do not be dismayed, for I am your God.
I will strengthen you and help you;
I will uphold you with my righteous right hand.

Isaiah 41:10

The Invitation

Precious one, I know that some days you feel all alone in your parenting journey. Nothing could be further from the truth. I am always with you. I will never, ever leave your side. My ears are open to your prayers, and My eyes are continually on you and your child. Just as I came to Hagar in the desert as the God who sees, I will come to you and sustain you. When feelings of loneliness overwhelm you, praise Me that I take you by the hand and gently remind you that I am with you. You are never alone! As you praise Me, My presence will envelop you, and I will reassure you of My nearness. Allow Me to breathe hope into your soul. Celebrate My glorious presence today. (Heb. 13:5; Gen. 16:13; Isa. 41:13; Ps. 139:7)

> I will not leave you as orphans; I will come
> to you. (John 14:18)

Parenting can feel incredibly lonely. But Jesus has promised that no matter who else may have forsaken us, He will never leave us. Today, focus your praise on His abiding presence. He is with you when you are up late at night rocking your baby or waiting for your teenager to arrive back home. God is with you when you are home all day with your toddler or driving your tween to and from various activities. He is with you when you are unsure of what to do and can't find anyone to process with. He will never, ever abandon you. As you praise Him for His constant presence, you will *feel* His presence more deeply.

Listen

Listen to "You're Not Alone" by Meredith Andrews, "Not Alone" by Jamie Grace, and "He Is with Us" by Love and the

Outcome. As you worship, praise Jesus as your Savior who never leaves your side. He is always with you.

Pray

Lord Jesus, there are moments on this parenting journey when I feel so alone. I praise You that my feelings don't determine the truth of Your abiding presence. I can confidently declare that You will never leave me and that You will never forsake me. Thank You for bending down and listening to every cry of my heart. You promise to be a father to the fatherless, to defend the cause of the widow, and to be faithful to the single parent. Even when my biological family isn't physically near me or emotionally supportive, You provide a family of faith around me that can give me the support I need. Thank You. I exult You, Lord Jesus, that You sent Your Spirit to live and dwell in me, which means I have a constant companion to help me parent at all hours of the day and night. Thank You that You help me daily with the burdens that come with parenting. You alone are everything I need. I will praise You in song today and glorify You with thanksgiving. (Heb. 13:5; Ps. 86:1 NLV; Ps. 68:5–6; Gen. 21:17–20; Ps. 68:19; Ps. 69:30)

Journal

Write a prayer to the Lord expressing any lonely feelings that you might have. Then choose one of the verses listed on this day of praise and write it out in your journal. Throughout the day, whenever you feel lonely, remind yourself of that verse. How might praising God reassure you of God's presence as you go throughout your day?

Day 9

But he said to me,
"My grace is sufficient for you,
for my power is made perfect in weakness."

2 Corinthians 12:9

The Invitation

I know how hard it is for you to face weakness in your child.
But I am God Almighty, the One who perfects power in weak-
ness. I delight in using your child's weaknesses to showcase My
strength. Every frailty in your child provides him the opportunity
for greater dependence on Me. Instead of trying to ignore or deny
his weaknesses, why not praise Me for them? Fix your eyes on Me
and not on more talented or "successful" children. Praise Me that
I will lead your child to live confidently through My Spirit. Praise
and thank Me that I will lead your child in triumph as he learns
deeper dependence on Me. Though My original disciples were not

extraordinary, I transformed them through the power of My Holy Spirit, and they became extraordinary world changers. Exalt and thank Me for what I will do as your child yields his weaknesses to Me. Watch and see what I will do as he yields his insufficiency to My all sufficiency! (2 Cor. 2:14; Acts 4:31; Isa. 66:19)

> In the same way, the Spirit helps us in our weakness. (Rom. 8:26)

It's difficult for parents to face weakness or limitations in their child. All parents want their child to be a "shining star." But God delights in using weaknesses for His glory and loves to shine through the shortcomings of His creation. Often those seeming imperfections become amazing strengths in God's kingdom. Dare to praise God today that weakness becomes strength in His hands.

Listen

Listen to "Blessings" by Laura Story and "Overcomer" by Mandisa. Allow the music to prompt your praise.

Pray

Lord Jesus, I worship You as the almighty Creator. By You all things were designed, things in heaven and on earth, visible and invisible. You created my child in perfect beauty and wisdom. You are not caught off guard by things such as physical limitations, emotional struggles, or learning disabilities. All my child's "weaknesses" can be matched with Your strength and used for Your glory. Thank You that while none of us are competent in ourselves, our competence comes from You, God. I praise You that I can speak words of confidence over my child, assuring him that Your strength is the perfect match for his weakness. I worship You, Lord, as the One who promises to give me wisdom and understanding about my child. Thank You that I can trust You to show me the best methods to assist my child in becoming all that You have called him to be. (Col. 1:16; 2 Cor. 3:5; 2 Tim. 2:7)

Journal

Today, think through the different challenges your child is facing (such as physical limitations, learning disabilities, sensory issues, Down syndrome, ADHD, and so on). God might be calling you to pray and ask for healing and wholeness, or He might be calling you to contentment. Either way, God can use your child's "weakness" to glorify Himself. Write a prayer of praise based on what you feel God is calling you to do.

Day 10

Come to me, all you who are weary and burdened,
and I will give you rest.

Matthew 11:28

The Invitation

My dear child, I see every dark circle under your eyes and hear
your every sigh. Whether you are up all night with an infant,
caring for a sick preschooler, or negotiating with a preteen, it's easy
to become weary. Even though you have no energy, I invite you to
praise Me. I am the One who is able to revive and restore you to
full energy. Create the space to pull away and rest in My presence.
When I lived on earth in a human body, I became tired; I even
fell asleep during a storm. I often withdrew to a quiet place so I
could spend time alone worshipping My Father. If I needed time
alone with God, how much more do you? Worship and praise Me
as you get up for a midnight feeding or get up early to drive your

child to a sports event. No moment spent praising Me is wasted. I know there are days when it feels like you will never catch up on sleep. During those seasons, snuggle down into My presence and worship Me. Learn to live life on two levels. On one level you can be feeding a baby or helping with homework, but on another level you can be celebrating My presence. As you choose to praise Me, I will revive and strengthen you! (Jer. 31:25; Mark 6:31; Luke 8:23; Mark 6:46; Mark 1:35; Luke 4:42)

> He will not grow tired or weary,
>> and his understanding no one can
>> fathom.
> He gives strength to the weary
>> and increases the power of the weak.
>> (Isa. 40:28–29)

Parents are on the job 24-7, which means you may not always get the rest you need. Today, in your tiredness, refresh yourself in the Lord. If possible, take a few moments for yourself. Take a bath, light a candle, turn on your praise music, and bask in God's presence. Allow Him to refresh and revive you as you praise Him.

Listen

Listen to "Worn" by Tenth Avenue North, "Come to Me" by Jamie Grace, and "Psalm 62" by Aaron Keyes. As you listen, allow yourself to simply rest. Don't pressure yourself to come up with a list of things to praise God for. Offer your rest as an offering of praise, and allow His Spirit to revive you.

Pray

I exalt You, Holy One! You promise that if I hope in the Lord, I will renew my strength. I will soar on wings like eagles; I will run and not grow weary, I will walk and not faint. I praise You, Lord Jesus, that You experienced tiredness and needed sleep while You were here on earth. Thank You for the understanding and grace You offer me when I feel dog tired. I praise and exalt You, Lord Jesus, for inviting me to rest and promising that I will find rest in You. Show me how to come to You for rest, even in the craziness of parenting. Thank You for the example You set of withdrawing and spending time in prayer. I praise You that as I worship You, Your Spirit will revive and refresh my weary soul. (Isa. 40:31; Jer. 6:16; Mark 6:31)

Journal

Think about the last time you were truly relaxed and rested. How did that affect you as a parent? How might you create even a tiny bit of space to be alone with God today and find rest in His presence?

Day 11

But each man has his own gift from God;
one has this gift, another has that.

1 Corinthians 7:7

The Invitation

*Beloved, I have created your child with unique gifts and talents. Seek to recognize the different abilities in your child so that you can nurture and encourage them. I long to reveal those talents to you. Praise Me in advance for how I will use your child's talents in the future. As you glorify Me for your child's talents and abilities—*_____ (list your child's talents and strengths in the blank)—*you will be able to affirm your child and bless her. As you exalt Me for the gifts I have given your child, you will be able to guide her more effectively in the way she should go. Consecrate each ability to Me. I am able to give you wisdom for how to ensure* *that those gifts flourish. As your child grows into adulthood, I will go before her and open doors so that the gifts I have given her can be utilized for My glory.* (Rom. 12:6; James 1:17; Prov. 22:6)

> Each one should use whatever gift he has received to serve others, faithfully administering God's grace in its various forms. (1 Peter 4:10)

It's essential for you to recognize and cultivate the talents God has given your child. As you praise God for giving your child gifts and abilities, He will open your eyes to all the ways He has blessed and equipped your child. For example, He may have given your child:

- Intellectual ability
- Strong verbal skills
- Artistic, creative, and/or theatrical abilities
- Musical talent
- Athleticism
- Perceptivity and insight

- Problem-solving skills
- Graciousness and the ability to make others feel welcome
- Compassion and mercy
- A strong sense of justice
- Leadership skills

Be intentional today about praising God for the specific gifts He has given your child. As you praise God, I believe the Holy Spirit will fill you with wisdom for how to best cultivate and nurture those gifts.

Listen

Listen to "Everything That's Beautiful" by Chris Tomlin and "The Proof of Your Love" by For King & Country. While you're listening, praise God for the unique gifts and talents He has given your child.

Pray

Lord Jesus, I praise You for the gifts and talents You have blessed my child with. Specifically, I praise You for her _____ (list your child's specific abilities and talents). *Thank You, Holy One, that Your Word teaches that the gifts and calling of God are irrevocable, which means no one can take away the talents and abilities that You have given my child. I worship You for the calling You have placed on my child's life, and I praise You in advance for how You will use my child's ability to* _____ (name a specific talent or gift) *in the future to help further Your kingdom. I worship You, Lord Jesus, as the giver of every good and perfect gift. Most of all, I praise You, God, that You offer my child the most indescribable gift through Your Son, Jesus Christ.* (Rom. 12:6; Rom. 11:29; James 1:17; 2 Cor. 9:15)

Journal

Spend a few moments thinking about the different talents and abilities God has given your child. Make a list of those abilities. How might praising God for those gifts help you be more effective at affirming and nurturing your child?

Day 12

As a father has compassion on his children,
so the LORD has compassion on those who fear him;
for he knows how we are formed,
he remembers that we are dust.

Psalm 103:13–14

The Invitation

As your Abba, I continually offer you grace. I know you sometimes feel angry and frustrated with your child. Anger isn't wrong, but it can be damaging if you don't contain it. Praising Me will strengthen your ability to be self-controlled. When you feel angry, lift your focus to Me. Gaze intently at My love and kindness. Remember, I know your humanness and patiently offer you compassion. When frustration overwhelms you or anger consumes you, take a moment to breathe. Bow your anger before Me. As you exalt Me for being your Father who is slow to anger and quick to forgive, I will help you to love your child in a similar fashion. As you praise Me, I will fill your heart with renewed love and understanding for your precious child. (Prov. 29:11; Ps. 103:8; 1 Cor. 13:5; Ps. 103:3; Col. 1:14)

> Love is patient, love is kind. It does not envy, it does not boast, it is not proud. It is not rude, it is not self-seeking, it is not easily angered, it keeps no record of wrongs.
> (1 Cor. 13:4–5)

Every parent feels frustrated and angry from time to time. However, God's desire for us as parents is that we not be "easily angered" (1 Cor. 13:5). The next time you are tempted to get mad at your child, pause, take a deep breath, and praise. With practice, this method of handling anger becomes easier. When we deal with our anger in this way, rather than passing on patterns of anger and rage, we leave a legacy of praise and grace. Today in your praise time, surrender to the Lord any unresolved anger toward your child. If you have some extra time, read through Psalm 103. Then praise God in advance for the renewed feelings of love He is going to give you for your child.

Listen

Listen to "One Hundred Three" by Antioch Live featuring James Mark Gulley, "How Deep the Father's Love for Us" by Phillips, Craig and Dean, and "Everlasting Father" by Elevation Worship. As you listen, praise God for how loving and gracious He is as a Father. Praise Him in advance for how He will transform any issues you have with anger.

Pray

Father, I praise You that You are not easily angered. Your Word teaches me that You "lavish" me with love. Thank You for always offering me grace, even when I fail. I desire to be like You, who consistently offers love, mercy, and grace to Your children, yet I find myself falling short. I praise You that You model loving-kindness as a parent. When I come to You, any anger I have toward my child seems to melt away in Your presence. Oh, Father, You are so incredibly good. I will exalt You today by controlling my anger and demonstrating Your compassion and kindness to my child. God, I believe that as I faithfully praise You, You will transform me to become more and more like You. Be glorified in my life, I pray. (Ps. 103:13; 1 John 3:1; 2 Cor. 3:18)

Journal

Think back to your childhood. What messages did you receive about anger? For example, were you told all anger was wrong? Or did you watch your parents scream at each other in an argument? How was anger demonstrated in your home? How might that impact your own parenting?

Day 13

You have made known to me the path of life;
you fill me with joy in your presence.

Psalm 16:11

The Invitation

My beloved child, worship Me as the only One who can give lasting joy to you and your child. As you praise and thank Me for being your joy giver, I will fill your heart with greater joy than you have ever known. A joyful heart is great medicine for the illness of taking life too seriously. As I transform you into a joyful parent, you will be able to more effectively model rejoicing for your child. You have the ability to set the emotional tone in your home. As you faithfully praise and thank Me for being the joy giver, I will ease tension in your home and fill it with laughter.

Exalt Me for taking great delight in your child and singing over him with joy. As I am singing, I will fill his heart with gladness. Thank Me that I look at your child with great pleasure and a sparkle in My eyes. As you praise Me, I will help your eyes to light up and your lips to smile. When you look at your child and beam, his heart is lifted. Celebrate My goodness! Worship and praise Me with gladness. Dance, sing, and rejoice. Don't be afraid of being silly. My heart loves exuberant worship. (Ps. 100:1–2; Zeph. 3:17; Neh. 8:10)

> He will yet fill your mouth with laughter
> and your lips with shouts of joy. (Job
> 8:21)

Today, praise Jesus for being the joy giver. Don't be afraid of playing loud and joyful music in your home. Figure out what music your child is drawn to and fill up your home with that style. Ask the Lord to fill you with so much joy that it spills over to the rest of your family. Celebrate throughout your day! If you have a toddler, get on the floor and play with him. If you have a grade school child, celebrate with a special after-school snack. If you have a teenager, go for a late night ice cream run. Let your child see the joy of the Lord displayed in your life.

Listen

Listen to "Happy Day" by Tim Hughes, "Shake" by MercyMe, and "God's Great Dance Floor" by Chris Tomlin. As you listen, imagine what it would be like to dance with the joy giver.

Pray

Lord Jesus, I praise You for being my joy giver, and my child's as well. Even babies in the womb feel joy. What an incredible blessing! Thank You that even though we experience suffering and sorrow, You are a God who plants joy in our hearts. Show me how to cultivate that joy in my child's life. I confess that it is far too easy for me to take life too seriously, yet You ordained laughter and celebration. I praise You that when You were here on earth, You went to parties and celebrations. As I praise You, Lord, I believe Your Holy Spirit will produce more joy in my life and that joy will spill into my child's life. Father, even though there are moments of weeping and sorrow, I praise You that there are also times of laughing and dancing. I praise You that You give my child moments of celebration, laughter, and gladness. As my child looks to You, You will fill his heart with laughter. (Luke 1:44; John 2:2; Job 8:21 ESV; Eccl. 3:4)

Journal

Is your home a happy place, filled with joy and laughter? Why or why not? Create a plan to celebrate tonight that God is the joy giver. You might make a special dinner or bake cupcakes. You might surprise your child by purchasing tickets to a sporting event. Be creative. Send your child the message that God is a joyful God and that He wants him to be filled with joy as well.

Day 14

Which of you, if his son asks for bread, will give him a stone?
Or if he asks for a fish, will give him a snake?
If you, then, though you are evil,
know how to give good gifts to your children,
how much more will your Father in heaven
give good gifts to those who ask him!

Matthew 7:9–11

The Invitation

Just as you love to give good gifts to your child, I love to give you good gifts as well. I am able to give exceedingly abundantly beyond all that you can ask or imagine. I know you sometimes worry about whether you can provide financially all that your child needs. Don't worry about what your family will eat or drink, or what you will wear, or how you will feed and clothe your child. I am the God of abundance. When worry tempts you, praise Me that I am aware of your child's every need. Thank Me in advance for My provision in her life. Don't be pulled into the world's way of thinking. Your child doesn't necessarily need the latest in toys, computer games, iPhones, and every other gadget out there. Don't set your heart on becoming wealthy or on giving your child every desire of her heart. As you seek Me above all else, I promise to provide what your child needs. You can trust Me; I will not fail you or your child. When you praise Me and fix your eyes on Me as the provider for your child, I will teach you contentment and your contentment will spill over to your child. (Eph. 3:20; Matt. 6:20–21; Matt. 6:33–34)

God himself will provide … (Gen. 22:8)

In this economy, with job losses and rising concerns over health care, it's easy to worry that we will not be able to provide for our kids. Our worry may drive us to set our sights on becoming wealthy. God's Word teaches us that He Himself will provide. When we praise Him for all that He has provided, it quiets our worry and nurtures contentment.

Listen

Listen to "God and King" by Antioch Live featuring Stephen Gulley and "You Crown the Year (Psalm 65:11)" by Hillsong Live. As you listen, praise God that He will faithfully provide for your family.

Pray

Lord God, I praise You that You promise to meet all my needs. Thank You for being a Father who delights in giving good gifts to Your children. Help me to set my eyes on You rather than impulsively chasing after the next job promotion so that I can provide more for my child. I praise You that You will show me if I need to add a second job, take a promotion, or creatively stretch the money to pay the bills. Just as Abraham told his son Isaac, help me to declare confidently to my child that You, Lord God, will provide. I praise You, Lord Jesus, that when You saw the need to feed the five thousand, You gave thanks in advance of the miracle. I long to thank You for Your promised provision even before I see it. I worship You, Lord Jesus, as my provider and as my child's provider. I put my trust in You and surrender every worry to You. (Phil. 4:19–20; Gen. 22:8; John 6:10–11)

Journal

Think about your family's financial needs. Make a list of each need. Then choose three of the verses referenced in this day of praise. Write out each verse as a prayer of praise over your financial situation.

Day 15

I am the good shepherd;
I know my sheep and my sheep know me—
just as the Father knows me and I know the Father—
and I lay down my life for the sheep.

John 10:14–15

The Invitation

Praise Me, My child. I am the Good Shepherd. I know your child completely, and I am able to lead him with gentleness and kindness. I have laid down My life for your child, taking the punishment for every sin he committed in the past and every sin he will commit in the future. When temptations threaten to steal and destroy your child's heart, I will not abandon him. If he strays away from faith, I will passionately and persistently pursue him. Your child is precious to Me, and I will keep chasing him until he comes home. Praise Me in advance for how I am able to bring your child back to Myself. Don't give up hope. And don't hold a grudge toward your child when he returns or stand back skeptically when he apologizes. Remember, there have been times when you have also strayed. When even one of My precious sheep returns home, heaven rejoices. As you exalt Me for never giving up on your child, I will pour resiliency into your fragile heart. Worship Me as the God who never gives up. Praising Me and thanking Me in advance keep hope alive. (John 10:11–15; Luke 15:4–7; Isa. 53:6)

> But while he was still a long way off, his father saw him and was filled with compassion for him; he ran to his son, threw his arms around him and kissed him. (Luke 15:20)

It is hard to praise God when your child is rebelling, wandering from faith, or making poor choices. But Jesus is the Good Shepherd who has not given up on your child. He will continuously pursue him. When you praise God in advance for the work that He is preparing to do in your child's life, spiritual victories are won. Today, praise God in advance for how He will bring your child back to faith and trust in Christ. If you are the parent of an infant or toddler, praise God that when your child walks through periods of disillusionment, doubt, or rebellion, the Good Shepherd will chase him until he returns to Him.

Listen

Today in your praise time, listen to "Glorious Ruins" by Hillsong, "It's Not Over" by Israel & New Breed, and "You Won't Relent" by Misty Edwards. As you listen, praise God for the work He is doing in your child's life. Thank Him that He is the Good Shepherd in your child's life.

Pray

Lord Jesus, I praise You as the Good Shepherd who knows my child completely. You know the temptations he faces every day. Father, You see his tendency toward _____
(name one or more specific sins that your child is prone toward: lying, cheating, stealing, overspending, addiction to drugs or alcohol, sexual promiscuity, or any other sinful

behavior). *I praise You that You are a God who never gives up. Thank You for illustrating Your heart for the prodigal in the story of the lost son. I exalt You, Holy One, that although You are holy, You consistently move toward the sinner. How amazing is Your pursuit of Your children! Though You are the Good Shepherd, You came as the sacrificial lamb to pay the price for our sin. I worship You, Lamb of God. Blessings, glory, and honor belong to You. I praise You that salvation belongs to You.* (John 10:10; Luke 15:11–32; Rev. 5:9, 12; Rev. 7:10)

Journal

Take some time today to reflect on Jesus as your child's Good Shepherd (John 10:1–18; Luke 15:1–7). What is the Holy Spirit speaking to you concerning your child? Write a prayer of praise exalting God as the Good Shepherd who is able to care for your child. If you have a child who has walked away from his faith, take some extra time today to study Luke 15:11–32. Read the passage slowly, several times. Write down anything you think the Holy Spirit may be speaking to you through this story.

Day 16

Teach us to number our days aright,
that we may gain a heart of wisdom.

Psalm 90:12

The Invitation

I know how often you feel there are not enough hours in the day.
Confusion over how to invest in quality time with your child
overwhelms you. Praise Me, My child, that I have ordained
twenty-four-hour days. I am the Alpha and Omega, and I hold
time in My almighty hands. When you feel inundated or torn
between tasks and spending time with your child, remember,
I, too, was bound to a twenty-four-hour day when I lived on
earth. I needed to create the space to eat, rest, be alone with the
Father, and continue ministry. Follow My example; when you
feel overwhelmed, pull away for moments of refreshment in My
presence. Worship Me as the One who can show you how to order

your day so that you can be fully present to your child but at the same time accomplish the tasks that need to be done and spend quality time with Me. Many tasks that you feel are priorities may not matter in twenty years. Your relationship with your child will matter. Invest in her life by playing with her, cheering her on, reading to her, praying over her, and praising Me for her. As you worship Me, I will help you prioritize your time. Don't follow the world's pattern of excess: excessive spending, excessive hours at work, excessive activities, excessive entertainment, and excessive time on social media. Instead, praise Me that I want to renew your mind and simplify your life. As you exalt Me, I will show you what is important. As a result, your family life will reflect My peace. (Rev. 1:17; Mark 1:35; Ps. 90:12; Rom. 12:2)

> What does a man get for all the toil and anxious striving with which he labors under the sun? (Eccl. 2:22)

Focus your praise time today on the fact that God is not pushing you to go faster and accomplish more. He is calling you to prioritize your busy schedule so that you have enough time each day to meet with Him, spend quality time with your child, and accomplish what needs to be done (career, household chores, and other responsibilities).

Listen

In your praise time today, listen to "The First and the Last" by Hillsong Live and "Be Still" by Bethel Music and Steffany Frizzell Gretzinger. As you worship, listen for the still, small voice of the Spirit.

Pray

Lord Jesus, I exalt You for being the great I AM who holds time in His hands. How I praise You that You Yourself were bound to twenty four hour days when You lived here on the earth and that You needed to sleep. Holy One, I feel so overwhelmed. When I look at the things I need to accomplish today, the activities I need to attend, and _____ (name any other pressing demands on your time), *it looks impossible. Lord, You said that I was not to work for food that spoils. Show me what this looks like on a practical level. I long to be like You, Jesus. You prioritized Your time with the Father, but You also made time for children. I confess that lately I am having difficulty finding time for both You and my child. Facebook, texting, email, and TV all seem to distract me from what's most important. Thank You that You are more than willing to show me how to structure my time. Lord, quiet the chaos in my soul. I praise You in advance that You will give me wisdom for how to unclutter my life in order to create more space for both You and my child. I exalt You as the One who calls me to live life unhurried and fully present to You. As I live attentive to You, I believe You will show me how to live more attentively to my child.* (John 8:56; Mark 4:38; John 6:27; Matt. 19:14; Ps. 46:10)

Journal

Spend a few minutes writing in your journal about how you spend your time. Think about these questions: How often do you check Facebook? How often are you on your smartphone? How often do you need to check email? How much time do you spend watching TV?

Here are a couple of suggestions for the rest of your day:

1. Fast from all social media today. Use the time you would normally spend on social

media to play with or join with your child in an activity.

2. Every time you feel tempted to check Facebook, Twitter, or other social media sites, praise God that He is fully present to your every need. Express your desire to be fully present to Him in return.

Day 17

Have I not commanded you?
Be strong and courageous.
Do not be terrified; do not be discouraged,
for the LORD your God will be with you wherever you go.

Joshua 1:9

The Invitation

Beloved, I know your heart feels heavy when your child walks
through seasons of fear, intimidation, or anxiety. Satan is your
child's enemy and will try to intimidate him with fear. Like every
bully, Satan is a coward. He will stumble and fall before Me.
Take up your position of authority as a parent and praise Me,
using My names to claim My power over your child's life. Sing
songs of praise to Me as you change your child's diaper or as you fix
lunches for school or do laundry. As you declare My goodness and
righteousness over your child, his fear and anxiety will diminish

under the authority of My name. In this way, you will be resist-
ing the devil on your child's behalf, and his faith will grow. As
you intentionally and consistently exalt Me, you will cultivate
an atmosphere of praise and worship in your home and model
praising Me to your child. (Eph. 6:12; Ps. 9:3; Phil. 2:10–11;
Ps. 47:6; James 4:7; Ps. 8:2)

> As they began to sing and praise, the LORD
> set ambushes against the men of Ammon
> and Moab and Mount Seir who were
> invading Judah, and they were defeated. (2
> Chron. 20:22)

Many children and teens struggle with anxiety and fear.
I believe Satan is using this weapon more and more to come
against our kids. Praising God defeats the enemy and assures
victory over fear in our lives and in our children's lives. When
you lift names of God over your family, Satan has to flee. So
in your praise time today, lift the names of our triune God
over your child's fear. For example, you might pray: *Lord Jesus,*
I exalt You because You are the almighty God and the Blessed
Controller of all things. I praise You that my child doesn't have to

fear _____ (put in a specific circumstance that your child feels afraid of). *You will always be his advocate.*

If you are unfamiliar with the names of God, here are some to get you started. (There is a more complete list of God's names on pages 175–80 in the "Taking It Further" section of this book.)

- Advocate—1 John 2:1
- Author of Our Faith—Hebrews 12:2
- Bread of Life—John 6:35
- Blessed Controller of All Things—1 Timothy 6:15 (PH)
- Counselor—Isaiah 9:6
- Deliverer—Romans 11:26
- Everlasting Father—Isaiah 9:6
- Good Shepherd—John 10:11
- Healer—Luke 5:30–31
- Immanuel (God with Us)—Matthew 1:23
- King of Kings—Revelation 19:16
- Lamb of God—John 1:29
- Light of the World—John 8:12

- Mighty God—Isaiah 9:6
- Prince of Peace—Isaiah 9:6

Listen

Listen to "Revelation Song" by Kari Jobe, "Great I Am" by Jared Anderson, and "Christ Is Risen" by Matt Maher. As you listen, exalt the names of God over your child. (If your child is young, you might kneel by his bed or crib and declare God's authority over his life as he sleeps.)

Pray

(This prayer in particular will be more meaningful if you refer to your child by name, so I encourage you to make it personal.)

Worthy are You, Lord Jesus, precious Lamb of God! You alone are deserving of all honor and glory. I praise You that all power, wisdom, and authority belong to You and that no weapon formed against my child will succeed. I worship You because You are a shield around my child. Thank You that when he is afraid, threatened, or bullied, he can call on Your name and put his trust in You. I praise You that You are his refuge and strength, an ever-present help in times of trouble. Thank You, Lord God Almighty, that because You are always near, my child does not have to fear. I praise You, Lord Jesus, that he can pray about everything and that as he gives thanks in all things, You will guard his heart from anxiety. I praise You now that You will envelop him with peace. (Rev. 5:12; Isa. 54:17; Ps. 7:10; Ps. 56:3; Ps. 46:1, 7; Phil. 4:6–7)

Journal

In what ways can you help your child battle fear? Make a list of as many ideas as possible (for example, teaching him to praise God, memorizing scriptures together, playing praise music in your home, and so on).

Day 18

For sin shall not be your master,
because you are not under law,
but under grace.

Romans 6:14

The Invitation

My child, I came to free those in captivity. Exalt Me as the only
One who can break the chains of addiction in your child's life.
When you become discouraged, praise Me that nothing, absolutely
nothing, is too difficult for Me. Thank Me that although you used
to be a slave to sin, My grace has set you free. I can do the same
for your child. Though your child may try to conceal her sin, I see
all. Thank Me that I desire truth in the innermost part of your
child's heart and can convict her conscience. Worship Me as the
God who is able to cleanse every sin and heal every addiction.
Although I may allow your child to experience the consequences

of her actions, I am the repairer of broken hearts and the restorer of broken lives. Instead of shame, I will bring grace to your child's life. I know you are weary, but don't give up on your child. I am the Messiah who rises with healing in His wings. As you persistently praise Me, I will restore your hope. (Isa. 61:1; Jer. 32:17; Rom. 6:17–18; Prov. 28:13; Isa. 58:12; Isa. 61:7; Mal. 4:2)

> But for you who revere my name, the sun
> of righteousness will rise with healing in its
> wings. (Mal. 4:2)

Today, praise God for His ability and desire to heal your child from any and every addiction. It is never too early to do this, even if your child is still an infant, toddler, or pre-schooler. If your child is already in slavery to an addiction, praise God for the freedom and healing He is able to bring. As you faithfully praise Him in advance for healing your child, I believe the enemy of addiction will be broken in your child's life. If you, as a parent, are struggling with an addiction or if you have in the past, praise God that He wants to heal you completely so that you don't pass any addictions down to your child.

Listen

Listen to "God Who Saves" by Antioch Live, "Where the Spirit of the Lord Is" by Hillsong Live, and "Hurricane" by Natalie Grant.

Pray

Lord Jesus, I feel so desperate for You today. I praise You that You bend down and listen to the cries of my heart. You see my child's tendency toward or addiction to _____ (name your child's addiction or tendency toward addiction; for example, people pleasing, lying, stealing, drugs, alcohol, video games, pornography, eating disorder, or any other addiction your child struggles with). *I praise You that You came to set the prisoner free. I know that You are opposed to denial. Your Word declares that You embody grace and truth and that You call us to truth. I praise You that You declare that if we face the truth, You will set us free. Father, thank You that I can trust You to show me what to do—whether I just need to continue praying or if I need to initiate an intervention or if I need to seek professional help on behalf of my child. Thank You that You have promised me that You will never stop pursuing my child no matter how often she runs back to* _____ (name the addiction). *As I wrestle with my sorrow and anxiety, I surrender my child into Your keeping. I praise You that You are a Father who disciplines only in love. Help me not to step in and rescue my child from the consequences of Your discipline. I choose this day to praise You by faith for the freedom You have promised my child. Thank You that You are completely able and willing to restore and heal.* (Ps. 86:1 NLT; Isa. 61:1; John 1:17; John 8:36)

Journal

Reflect back on your life as a teenager and young adult. Did you struggle with any addictions? If you are married, did your spouse struggle with any addictions? If so, what led you to freedom? What led your spouse to freedom? Write a prayer of praise for the freedom Christ gave you and for the freedom He wants to bring to your child.

Day 19

If you have faith
as small as a mustard seed,
you can say to this mountain,
"Move from here to there"
and it will move.
Nothing will be impossible for you.

Matthew 17:20

The Invitation

Dear one, fix your eyes on Me. I am the author and perfecter of faith. I know how scary it feels when your child begins to doubt his faith. You are left wondering, Will he walk away from the Truth? *When doubts surface, don't freak out. Instead, listen. If you panic, your child may stop talking to you, and you will have missed the opportunity to help him process his beliefs. Learn to live life on two levels. On one level you can be listening to your child;*

on another you can be praising Me for the wisdom I will give you in the conversation. Remember that everyone has doubts. Don't present to your child a false view of yourself, as though you have never had a doubt in your life. Instead, be authentic and humble like the father who said to Jesus, "I do believe; help me overcome my unbelief!" Express your desire for Me to increase your faith as well as your child's. Exalt Me for the opportunities I am providing for your child's faith to grow and flourish. His faith journey will have ups and downs and twists and turns. Understand that he is being bombarded every day with false messages from society and the evil one. Wrestling is part of the journey. As you praise Me faithfully and model consistency, you will help hold up the shield of faith over your child's heart. (Heb. 12:2; Mark 9:24; Eph. 6:16)

We live by faith, not by sight. (2 Cor. 5:7)

Today, praise God as the author and perfecter of faith and for continually providing opportunities for your child's faith to grow. As you praise God today, you might pray passages from the book of Ephesians, inserting your child's name when applicable. For example: *"Praise be to the God and Father of our*

Lord Jesus Christ, who has blessed _____ *in the heavenly realms with every spiritual blessing"* (Eph. 1:3). The following passages can be used in this way. I once did this on behalf of one of my children for a month, and God honored my efforts beyond what I had imagined.

- Ephesians 1:3–9
- Ephesians 1:11–14
- Ephesians 1:17–19
- Ephesians 2:4–5
- Ephesians 2:8–10
- Ephesians 2:13–14
- Ephesians 2:18
- Ephesians 3:14–20
- Ephesians 4:14–15
- Ephesians 6:10–18

Listen

Listen to "Give Me Faith" by Elevation Worship, "King of Heaven" by Paul Baloche, and "Holding On" by Jamie Grace. As you listen, praise God that your child's faith doesn't depend on his ability to hold on to God's hand, but on God's ability to hold on to his.

Pray

I praise You, God, the Father of the Lord Jesus Christ, because You chose my child before the foundation of the earth to be Your precious child. I thank You that You set Your affection on him and set him apart for Your purpose. I praise You that my child has forgiveness through Your blood. Your Word declares that if he has confessed with his mouth and believed in his heart that God raised Jesus from the dead, then he will be saved. Thank You for Your promise that You will complete the good work You began in him. I praise You that my child's doubt cannot prevent Your plan from being accomplished in his life. You say that faith comes from hearing the message and that the message is heard through the word of Christ. Thank You that You will repeatedly present opportunities for my child to hear Your voice and for his faith to grow. Holy One, some of those opportunities may come in the form of difficulties. When You allow him to experience suffering, help me to trust You and not lean on my own understanding. Help me not to step in and save him from those difficulties but to praise You in advance for how You're using those circumstances to strengthen his trust and faith in You and Your goodness. (Eph. 1:4; Rom. 10:9; Phil. 1:6; Rom. 10:17; Prov. 3:5–6)

Journal

Make a time line of your child's progression in faith. Note experiences of faith that stand out to you, such as asking Jesus into his heart, baptism, confession of faith, a pivotal prayer, or any other marker that seems significant in his spiritual journey. Write a prayer of praise for each of these events. The time line can be a symbol of hope when it appears your child is having moments or seasons of doubt.

(If you have a young adult child who is struggling with his faith, I recommend giving him Philip Yancey's book *Reaching for the Invisible God*. It is an excellent resource for both parent and child. You might both read it and then discuss it together.)

Day 20

But the Counselor,
the Holy Spirit,
whom the Father will send in my name,
will teach you all things
and will remind you of everything I have said to you.

John 14:26

The Invitation

Be assured, precious one, if your child has received Me as her Savior, she has the Spirit of the living God dwelling in her. I left My Spirit to dwell in human hearts, even the hearts of children. When your child accepts Jesus as Savior, immediately begin praising Me that My Spirit lives and dwells in your child and that My Spirit, the Counselor, is available to your child 24-7. My Spirit teaches, convicts, cleanses, strengthens, and reveals the things of God to your child's heart. Praise Me for this amazing gift. My Spirit is the greatest change agent your child has. I, through the power of My Spirit, changed the lives of My disciples and transformed them into bold men of God, and I am able to do the same in your child's life. Worship and exalt Me. Ask Me to fill your child, awakening in her a deeper awareness of My presence and power. (John 14:16; John 14:26; Rom. 15:16; Rom. 8:23; Eph. 3:16; 1 Cor. 2:10; Acts 4:31)

> Having believed, you were marked in him with a seal, the promised Holy Spirit. (Eph. 1:13)

Isn't it encouraging to know that your child has the Holy Spirit living in her? Personalize your praise for the work of the Holy Spirit in your child's life by inserting her name in the blanks below. Praise God today that:

- The Holy Spirit is _____'s counselor (John 14:26).
- The Holy Spirit teaches _____ and leads her into truth (John 14:16–17).

- The Holy Spirit convicts _____ of sin (John 16:8).
- The Holy Spirit guides _____ (John 16:13).
- The Holy Spirit reassures _____ that she is God's child (Rom. 8:16).
- The Holy Spirit helps _____ to pray (Rom. 8:23).
- The Holy Spirit strengthens _____ when she is weak (Rom. 8:26; Eph. 3:16).
- The Holy Spirit brings _____ hope (Rom. 15:13).
- The Holy Spirit reveals deeper truth about God to _____ (1 Cor. 2:10).
- The Holy Spirit gives _____ special gifts (Heb. 2:4).

Listen

Today in your praise time, listen to "Fall Afresh" by Bethel Music and Jeremy Riddle, "Spirit Speaks" by All Sons & Daughters, and "Breathe On Us" by Kari Jobe. As you praise

Jesus for leaving His Spirit, ask Him to fall afresh on your child's heart.

Pray

Lord Jesus, I praise and exalt You for leaving Your Spirit. What an amazing gift! Your presence dwells in us 24-7. Thank You that Your Spirit is also available and able to dwell in my child. I praise You that when my child accepted You as her Savior, Your Spirit came to live in her.* I praise You in advance for how Your Spirit will lead, guide, convict, renew, and strengthen my child. Holy Spirit, I thank You that when my child feels fearful, You will provide courage and boldness, just as You did for the disciples. Thank You that as my child yields to Your Spirit, You will change her into a godly person. I exalt You, God, that Your desire is to transform my child into the image of Your Son, Jesus Christ, through the power of Your almighty Spirit. (John 14:16–17; 2 Cor. 3:18)

Journal

Look back over the list of ways the Holy Spirit can help your child. Which of these would be the most helpful in your child's life at this time? Why? What do you think the Holy Spirit is saying to you today about how you might help your child develop a deeper understanding of the Holy Spirit's role and function in her life?

*If your child has not yet accepted Christ as Savior, praise God that the Holy Spirit is continuously pursuing your child's heart. His desire is that your child place her faith and trust in Jesus as Savior and Lord of her life.

Day 21

He who walks with the wise grows wise.

Proverbs 13:20

The Invitation

Friendships are an important part of a happy and healthy life. Praise Me that I designed your child as a relational being with the longing for friendship. When I walked this earth, I enjoyed close friendships, and I want My children to enjoy them as well. Praise Me that friendship was My idea in the first place. Exalt Me, beloved parent, that I am able to give your child discernment in the realm of friendships. Thank Me that My desire is to have your child walk with the wise. I know there are times when you grow concerned about the influence friends might be having on your child. As you continually bow before Me, I will give you discernment for how to guide your child toward healthy friendships. Stay engaged, and seek to know his friends. If you feel a certain relationship is destructive, praise Me in advance for the wisdom I will give you. Not all friendships will be ideal, but I am able to teach your child lifelong lessons, even through challenging relationships. I have called your child to be salt and light. As he seeks to honor Me, I will show him how to exemplify love and point his friends to Me. Praise Me in advance for the way I will use him for My glory.

Thank Me that your home can be used as a place to nurture your child's confidence in making friends. When you notice your child making wise choices as he develops his social circles, affirm him. As you affirm him, he will be more inclined to continue to foster healthy friendships. Praise Me that as your child seeks Me, I will be his confidence and guard him from being snared by friends who might corrupt. (Prov. 3:21; Prov. 4:11; Matt. 5:13–14; Prov. 3:26)

> The godly give good advice to their friends; the wicked lead them astray. (Prov. 12:26 NLT)

Praise God for your child's friends, as well as for the discernment God is able to give him in forming those friendships. Help your child nurture friendships with people who will encourage him to walk with God, as well as friendships with nonbelieving friends who will challenge him to share his faith. Both are important pieces of his spiritual development.

During your praise time today, focus on God's ability to give both you and your child discernment in the realm of his friendships. If you feel uncomfortable with one of your child's friends, ask God for wisdom, thanking Him in advance for the wisdom He will give you. Continue to praise Him until He gives you wisdom about what to do. Praising God will open your ears to hear the soft voice of the Holy Spirit.

Listen

Listen to "Friend of God" by Phillips, Craig and Dean, "Love Goes On" by Hillsong Young & Free, and "Show Jesus" by Jamie Grace. As you worship, praise God that He offers friendship to your child. Then praise Him for your child's friends and that He is able to shine through your child to show Jesus to others.

Pray

Lord Jesus, I exalt You for creating my child with the deep desire for friendship. I praise You because You are a relational God. I praise You that when You lived here on earth, You modeled friendship. You attended weddings, went to dinner parties, and hung out with close friends. Holy One, I praise You for _____, _____, *and* _____ (name your child's friends) *who bring great joy to my child's life. But, Father, I feel concerned about* _____ *and* _____ (names of friends), *who I worry are having a bad influence on my child. Holy Spirit, I praise You that You are my counselor. I praise You that You promise that if I ask, You will give me wisdom. Show me what it looks like today to pour confidence into my child in the realm of friendships. Lord, I bow before You and ask You that if I have a critical spirit toward any of my child's friends, that You will reveal that to me. I praise You, Father, that Your ultimate goal in my life and in the life of my child is that we glorify You and be transformed into the image of Your Son, Jesus Christ.* (John 2:1; John 15:14; John 14:16; James 1:5; 2 Cor. 3:18)

Journal

Think through your child's friendships. Write down the names of three friends for whom you feel especially thankful. Write down some of the reasons you are thankful for these friends. Then take some extra time today and write each of those three friends a special note, thanking him or her for being such a good friend to your child.

Day 22

This I call to mind
and therefore I have hope:
Because of the LORD's great love
we are not consumed,
for his compassions never fail.
They are new every morning;
great is your faithfulness.

Lamentations 3:21–23

The Invitation

My beloved, I know how your heart aches when your child walks through deep disappointment and loss. My heart was torn in two as I watched My Son as He was betrayed and then crucified. I know it may feel as though I have forgotten your child, but take heart. Remind yourself that My great love and mercy will never fail her. I know the plans I have for your child, plans to prosper her and not harm her, plans to give her a hope and a future. When your child faces disappointment or devastating loss, will you dare to praise Me? Will you bow down before Me and praise Me that I will fulfill My purpose for your child? Exalt Me by faith that I will not abandon her. As you put your hope in Me, praise Me for the hope I am able to pour into your child's broken heart. Though it may feel as if her grief will never end, sorrow only lasts for a time, and joy will come again. Praise Me that, as your child delights in Me, I will give her the desires of her heart. (Lam. 3:21–22; Jer. 29:11; Ps. 138:2, 8; Ps. 42:5; Ps. 30:5; Ps. 37:4)

> The LORD is close to the brokenhearted
> and saves those who are crushed in spirit.
> (Ps. 34:18)

It is difficult for a parent to watch a child experience sorrow and loss. It can feel even more painful for you, the parent, than it does for your child. If, when your child desperately needs hope, you dare to praise God above your child's sorrow, God will honor those praises. I believe that your worship lifts a protective shield of praise over your child's aching heart.

Now, I must give a word of warning here. *Don't preach at your child or spout easy answers.* Feel with her, grieve with her, but praise God in the privacy of your own worship. It can be helpful to build an "emergency scripture kit" that you can use in your praise time when your child is walking through sorrow. Your emergency scripture kit will include four to five verses that you have memorized and that remind you that God is the hope giver. I have done this, and it has proven invaluable. Here are a few of my favorites:

- Psalm 34:1–2, 18
- Psalm 39:7
- Psalm 42:5
- Lamentations 3:21–24
- Romans 15:13
- 1 Corinthians 15:19
- 2 Corinthians 4:18

Listen

Today in your praise time, listen to "Need You Now (How Many Times)" by Plumb, "Cornerstone" by Hillsong Live, and "Anchor" by Hillsong Live.

Pray

Abba, how I praise You that You understand every ache in my heart. Thank You for giving up Your beloved Son so that abundant life might be restored. Lord Jesus, I praise You that You carried my child's sorrows in Your heart as You hung on the cross. I exalt You that by Your wounds, my child is healed. I worship You for such amazing love. Thank You for promising to be close to the brokenhearted.

Lord, I praise You that Your Word teaches me that suffering produces perseverance in my child's life. And perseverance builds character, and character leads to hope. Holy One, I pray that my child will someday find the courage to declare confidently with Job, "Though he slay me, yet will I hope in him." Until that time, Lord, I commit to holding on to hope on behalf of my child. You alone are the giver of hope.

I worship You! (Isa. 53:4–5; Ps. 34:18; Rom. 5:3–4; Job 13:15)

Journal

Look over the verses listed as possible "emergency verses." Choose one. Write the verse in your journal, and then write about why you chose that verse and what it means to you. Then write the verse on an index card, and put it in a place in your home where you will see it often. Commit the verse to memory.

Day 23

For we are God's workmanship,
created in Christ Jesus to do good works,
which God prepared in advance for us to do.

Ephesians 2.10

The Invitation

I created your child to live life with purpose and meaning. His life is a beautiful poem that brings honor to My name. Exalt Me! I am glorified as your child discovers his unique calling. Many parents hold tight to their children, preventing them from becoming all I have intended. Beloved, don't make that mistake. I know the plans I have for your child. I have placed a holy calling on his life that might be different from what you envisioned. When you are tempted to direct your child toward your plans for his life, stop. Beloved parent, trust Me and move out of the way. Surrender your dreams and desires. Allow Me the freedom to guide your precious one into the vision I have for his life. As he seeks My face, I will direct his paths and lead him to live life intentionally and purposefully for My glory. Praise Me in advance for the distinct calling I have given him. As he grows and develops, praise Me that I am able to cultivate a deep sense of purpose in his heart. Remember, his supreme purpose is not to make you happy but to glorify Me, the Lord Jesus Christ. (Eph. 2:10; Jer. 29:11; Prov. 3:5–6; 1 Peter 2:9; 2 Thess. 1:11–12)

I urge you to live a life worthy of the calling
you have received. (Eph. 4:1)

I have met many parents who have discouraged their children from going into ministry because the salary and benefits are often lower than what is offered in other professions. I have met others who have discouraged their children from accepting a job that the child felt was from God because the parent wanted the child to live close to home. Dear parent, God is the only One who has the right to set the course of your child's life. Your job is to encourage your child to be all that God has called him to be and to applaud his efforts to follow God's calling. When you surrender your dreams for your child and praise God that His dreams are always best, you are able to move out of the way. Praising God quiets your desire for control. In your praise time today, surrender every dream you have for your child and exalt God that His plans and purpose for your child are best.

Listen

Listen to "My God" by Desperation Band and "My Hope" by Paul Baloche. As you listen, praise God that He will empower you to let go and surrender your dreams for your child. Exalt Him that He will give your child purpose as your child seeks Him. Then listen to "Born for This (Esther)" by Mandisa. As you listen, praise God that His calling for your child's life is incredible. Praise Him that as your child seeks Him, He will unveil His vision for your child's life.

Pray

Lord Jesus, I exalt You as Lord over all. I praise You that You created my child for Your glory and that You have a specific purpose and plan for his life. You have invited him to glorify You, to become more Christlike, and to join You in Your vision for the world. What an amazing honor to be able to partner with You in bringing others to Your love!

God, my heart feels overwhelmed when I think of how You might use my child for Your kingdom. I praise You that as he seeks to honor You, You will provide vision for his life. Thank You that as You reveal that vision, You will enable him to step out in courage like You empowered Esther in the Old Testament. I worship You, Lord, because You are the One who calls my child, and You will remain faithful to work through him. Thank You that I don't need to worry or try to set the course of my child's life. You are more than able to call and empower. I only need to let go. How I worship You, almighty God! (Rev. 19:16; Ps. 149:4; Est 4:14; 1 Thess. 5:24)

Journal

Think through the concept of letting go. What do you think it means to "let go" in a God-honoring fashion? What emotions does letting go stir up in you? What do you think God is calling you to do?

Day 24

Blessed are those who hunger and thirst
for righteousness,
for they will be filled.

Matthew 5:6

The Invitation

Precious parent, your child is hungry and thirsty for so many things: love, affection, affirmation, and friendship. Those needs are not wrong; I designed them. Though you can provide some of those gifts for your child, I am the only One who can meet her deepest longings. I crafted your child's heart with a hunger that only I can satisfy. Your materialistic culture tells you that you can give your child everything she desires. But this is not true. Only I am able to meet the deepest soul cravings of the heart. Praise Me as your child's Bread of Life and Living Water. Worship Me as the One who can quench your child's thirst. As your child hungers for

Me, I will satisfy her. I am the Lord God Almighty who fills the hungry with good things. Exalt Me! As you worship Me, you will be modeling the deep gratification only found in My presence. As you adore Me for being the only One who can satisfy your child's longings, I will remind you that you cannot be God to your child. Bow before Me and praise Me that I alone am God. This will eliminate any inclination that you might have toward setting yourself up as "God" in your home. (John 6:35; John 7:37; Ps. 107:9; Ps. 63:1; Isa. 42:8)

> Come, all you who are thirsty,
>> come to the waters;
> and you who have no money,
>> come, buy and eat! (Isa. 55:1)

One of the greatest temptations we face as parents is thinking that we can be everything to our children. But we cannot possibly satisfy their every need. Only God can do that. Spend your praise time today acknowledging that He alone can satisfy the deepest longings of your child's heart. As you praise Him, the Holy Spirit will quiet your urge to try to be everything to your child.

Listen

Listen to "Come to the Water" by Kristian Stanfill and "My Soul Longs for You" by Misty Edwards.

Pray

Lord Jesus, I worship and exalt You for being the Bread of Life and Living Water. Thank You for creating my child with deep longings that only You can fill. How I praise You that as my child comes to You, You will satisfy her with Yourself. Only Your presence can fill the gaping holes in her heart. I confess that at times I have tried to meet every desire of my child's heart. Oh, Holy One, forgive me. I thank You that as a human parent I am unable to fulfill every hunger of her heart. If I could, then my heart would become proud, and I would forget how much I need You in my parenting journey. I exalt You alone as God. Help me to worship You often as the only One completely able to satisfy.

Lord, thank You that Your Word promises that as Your children set their hearts on You, You will fulfill their desires. I praise You for the abundant satisfaction You have promised. Take my child deeper into knowing this truth. Help her to feel the deep gratification of experiencing Your presence. Bread of Life, I bow before You as the only One who can completely satisfy, and I ask You to increase my child's appetite for You. I praise You in advance for how You will do this. (John 6:35; John 7:37; Jer. 31:14; Ps. 37:4; Deut. 8:12–14)

Journal

What soul cravings have you noticed in your child? How might your child's life look different if she went to God to meet those hunger needs? What did God speak to you today?

Day 25

Blessed are the peacemakers,
for they will be called sons of God.

Matthew 5:9

The Invitation

My child, some of the happiest people on earth are those who have learned to forgive. I want you and your child to feel joyful and free. Unforgiveness tortures and imprisons the soul. Praise Me that I have called your child to be a peacemaker: one who offers forgiveness and mercy to others. When others hurt your child, you will feel angry, just as he will, but you must model moving beyond the anger to forgiveness. Surrender to Me your anger and desire for vengeance. Meditate on My forgiving nature. I have separated your sins as far as the east is from the west. Praise and exalt Me as the giver of grace. Worship Me because I call your child to love his enemies and to pray for those who hurt him. Exalt Me for how I will empower your child to do the impossible—to forgive his enemies.

Too many parents judge and condemn others. As a result, their children also judge and condemn. Don't fall into this pit of destruction. Instead, worship Me as the One who continually offers grace and mercy. As you faithfully praise Me, I will mold your heart so that it becomes more like Mine. As you faithfully model grace and mercy, your child will follow your lead. My desire is that he will continually forgive and not pass judgment on others. In this day of bullying and cruelty, I am calling My children to live a life of mercy and love. (Matt. 18:35; Matt. 5:9; Ps. 103:12; Matt. 5:44; Rom. 14:10)

> Therefore let us stop passing judgment on one another. (Rom. 14:13)

One of my regrets as a parent is that too often I modeled a judgmental spirit rather than a merciful spirit, especially when it came to those who hurt my family. I wanted to validate my children's feelings, but at times I went too far. As God began to change my life through my intentional times of praise, He called me specifically to lay down my judgmental spirit. As I worshipped the grace giver, He called me to forgive, even those who hurt my children. I'm not going to lie; it wasn't easy! But as I purposefully and faithfully surrendered each person who hurt my children, I began to experience new freedom. That same freedom is available to you.

Today in your praise time, focus on God as the grace giver. Worship Him for the grace He has extended to you. Tell Jesus that you want to be more like Him and that you want to model grace for your children. As you worship Him, surrender any unforgiveness or bitterness toward any person who has hurt your child. Praise Him that He is also calling your child on a journey of forgiveness.

Listen

Listen to "Search My Heart" by Hillsong United and "Come Thou Fount of Every Blessing" by Sara Groves. As you listen, ask the Holy Spirit to reveal any judgmental or unforgiving spirit in you.

Pray

I exalt You, Lord Jesus, because You are the ultimate peacemaker. You orchestrated peace between a holy God and sinful humanity with Your death and resurrection. How I worship You that You consistently offer me forgiveness. I know that I have no right to pass judgment on anyone else because I also am a sinner. Thank You that Your kind offer of grace leads me to repentance. Holy Spirit, search my heart and reveal to me any judgmental or critical spirit. Create in me a clean heart. Show me anyone whom I need to forgive. Instead of using my mouth to judge others, let me use my mouth to declare Your praises.

I praise You, Lord, that You invite my child to follow Your example and become a peacemaker. Thank You that You want him to be free from all bitterness and resentment so that he might walk in the freedom of forgiveness. I worship You, Lord Jesus, for giving my child many opportunities to practice extending grace to others. Thank You for what You are doing in his life. I praise You that as he surrenders his hurt and pain to You, You will fill him with comfort and peace. I praise You in advance for how You will use him in the future to comfort others who walk a similar journey. (Rom. 2:1; Rom. 2:4; Ps. 51:10, 15; Eph. 4:31–32; 2 Cor. 1:3–4)

Journal

If possible, take a few extra minutes today. Sit quietly and ask the Holy Spirit to search your heart. Ask Him to reveal the name of anyone you need to forgive. Then write out a prayer in your journal asking God to bless the person who has hurt you or your child. Then think through your child's friendships or acquaintances. Is there anyone you can think of whom your child might be struggling to forgive? If so, ask the Lord to create in your child's heart a willing spirit. Then write a prayer of praise to the Lord for how He will use the hurtful situation in your child's life in the future.

Day 26

Whether you turn to the right or to the left,
your ears will hear a voice behind you, saying,
"This is the way; walk in it."

Isaiah 30:21

The Invitation

Praise and exalt Me for being the God who goes before and pre-
pares the way for those who follow Me. I know you worry about
your child's future, particularly about whom and if your child
will marry. When your mind begins to worry, praise Me instead.
I am the God who is already in tomorrow. I am the same God
who went before Abraham's servant to find a wife for Isaac. Just as
I went before him, I am able to go before your child. I will stand
watch over her even as she marries and begins to build her home.
If your child remains single, I will surround her with My sover-
eign love. Beloved, your worry doesn't accomplish anything except

creating knots in your stomach. When you allow your mind to worry unrestrained, you imagine situations that I never ordained you to walk through. Trust Me. Pray for your child's future mate, and praise Me in advance for how I am shaping that person now. Prayer and praise are like two boxing gloves against worry. If you faithfully pray and praise Me, you will experience far less anxiety. (Gen. 24:7–8; Ps. 127:1; Phil. 4:6)

> Search me, O God, and know my heart;
> test me and know my anxious
> thoughts. (Ps. 139:23)

When I asked friends what they worry about as parents, one of the leading responses was whom their child might marry. I know that place of worry. When I was raising my kids, I worried quite a bit about whom they would marry. When they were very young, I began praying for their future mates. As I grew in my love of praise, I also began praising God in advance for their future spouses. My praise was an act of faith. Now, all four of my children are married, and I love each of their spouses! Did my praising God affect my children's choice of spouse, or did my praising God prepare me so that I would love my children's spouses? Maybe I'll ask God that when I get to heaven. I can't guarantee that if you praise God for your child's future spouse you will love that person, but I can tell you that God honors praise and praising Him in advance prepares your heart for what He intends to do.

Today, praise God intentionally for your child's future spouse. Bow before the One who is sovereign, and praise Him that if He calls your child to be single, you will trust that as best. I believe that when we choose to praise God by faith, God honors our decision.

Listen

Today, listen to "Oh How I Need You" by All Sons & Daughters and "You Never Fail" by Hillsong Live. As you listen, praise God that you do not have to worry. He will meet you as you seek Him, and He never fails.

Pray

Sovereign Lord, I praise You because You are already in tomorrow. I exalt You for being not only great in Your sovereignty but also good in Your sovereignty. Thank You that Your purposes are always good. I worship You, Lord. I bow down before You and lay every anxiety at Your feet. I declare by faith, "I trust You." My days and the days of my child are in Your hands. Holy One, I don't always understand Your ways. I don't understand how You move in response to my prayers or to my praise. I simply know that You call me to praise You and You honor those who praise You. So accept my humble praise. I praise You by faith for my child's spouse. Thank You that this very moment You are at work in that person's life. (If your child is married, name the spouse.) Father, I praise You for the opportunities You will give me to show love and acceptance. I long to grow deeper into being a parent who trusts You. Thank You for the picture You gave me in your Word of being like a tree firmly planted by rivers of water that doesn't worry about drought or storm. Help me gradually become a strong and steady parent who doesn't worry. (Ps. 31:19; Jer. 32:19; Ps. 31:15; Jer. 17:8)

Journal

Today in your journal, answer this question: What is your biggest worry concerning your child's future marriage and/or spouse? Then write a prayer of praise to the Lord that He never fails and He is already in the future. If your child is already married, make a list of qualities of her spouse for which you are thankful.

Day 27

I am the LORD, who heals you.

Exodus 15:26

The Invitation

Precious parent, I know how scary it feels when your child is sick. I am the holy healer. As you cry out to Me, exalt Me. I am capable of healing every disease your child might develop. Bow before Me and praise Me for the wisdom I will give you as you contemplate when to take your child to the doctor. I am the God who hears your prayers and sees your tears. Praise Me that I am your Savior who rises with healing in His wings.

I know that you are tempted to doubt My goodness when I am not healing your child as you hope. I understand the crisis of your faith because I am ever mindful that you are only human, but I long for you to trust Me. Declare by faith, "I trust You, Lord." When you bow before Me with open hands, releasing your child into My healing hands, I am so proud of you! Whether I heal your child here and now or in heaven, I am the Lord who heals. When you praise Me even though you don't understand My ways, I am glorified and your faith is bolstered. (Exod. 15:26; Ps. 103:3; 2 Kings 20:5; Mal. 4:2; Ps. 103:14)

> "I will restore you to health and heal your wounds," declares the LORD. (Jer. 30:17)

A pivotal choice in my parenting journey was the night I got on my knees next to my cot in a hospital in Kenya, Africa. Our eighteen-month-old daughter lay deathly ill from an African virus. That night, through many tears, I prayed, *Lord, I love this baby girl so much. But I know You love her even more than I do. Whether You heal her or take her to heaven to be with You, I will choose to praise You.*

The choice to surrender my daughter was pivotal, because it set the stage for the rest of my parenting journey. While God did heal my daughter, in the years that followed, He invited me many times to surrender my hopes and desires in favor of His. The Lord instructs us to pray for healing but also to trust Him with the outcome. Although Christ can bring healing, not all sickness and disabilities are healed in this life-time. However, when we intentionally choose to praise God whether He heals or not, our faith grows.

Today, praise God that He is the holy healer. Declare by faith that you trust Him to heal your child as He feels is best. Surrender is an act of worship that you will repeat many times in your parenting journey. Today, once again, as an act of worship, surrender your child into His almighty, healing hands.

Listen

Listen to "I Surrender" by Hillsong Live and "Even If (The Healing Doesn't Come)" by Kutless. As you listen, praise God that you can trust Him and surrender your child to Him.

Pray

Lord Jesus, I praise and exalt You as the holy healer. I worship You because You have a heart for parents with sick children and You delight in healing children for the glory of Your name. Thank You that no illness has authority over my child's body. I worship You alone as Lord over his body, soul, and spirit. Thank

You that You invite me to pray for healing and that You hear the cries of my heart. I praise You, Father, that You instruct me to call on the elders of my church to pray for healing. I praise You for the many times in the past when You have healed my child from _____ (name specific illnesses that God has healed your child from: asthma attacks, flu, croup, appendicitis, and so on). *I worship You, Lord Jesus, as the One who knows what is best for my child. I bow before You. I open my hands and surrender my precious child into Your almighty, healing hands.* (Luke 8:41–56; James 5:14; Isa. 59:1)

Journal

Take a little extra time today and read Luke 8:41–56. Then write down anything you feel God is speaking to you.

Day 28

Be devoted to one another in brotherly love.
Honor one another above yourselves.

Romans 12:10

The Invitation

I have created your family to be a picture of the loving community that exists within the Trinity. Just as We—God the Father, God the Son, and God the Holy Spirit—exist in loving fellowship, so I have designed your family to live in loving relationship. My desire is that your child enjoys deep community with each member of your family. The relationships within your family, and even within your extended family, are strengthened as you, the parent, make praise and worship a priority. As you praise Me, I am able to strengthen your relationship with your child. As a result, the relationships between your child and any siblings will also strengthen. Beware, My precious child, because the enemy of your soul wants to destroy the relationships in your family. He understands that a house divided against itself will fall to ruin. However, a house built on genuine worship and praise will have a far greater chance of withstanding the storms of life. Praise Me with a genuine heart, and teach your children to praise Me as well. When conflict arises, praise Me that I will give you wisdom as to how to best encourage peace. When you bow before Me and worship, I will break patterns of harshness within your family. As you exalt Me, I will empower you to confess your faults and apologize when you have wronged your child. In this way, you will be setting an example of how to apologize and ask forgive-ness. As your child grows, she is more likely to praise Me and to value her relationships with family members. As you exalt Me, I will make your home a safe refuge for your family and for others. (Luke 11:17; Luke 6:48–49; Eph. 6:4; Prov. 14:26)

> The wise [parent] builds her house, but with her own hands the foolish one tears hers down. (Prov. 14:1)

Many parents I've talked with have expressed a deep desire for their family to be close and have asked Steve and me about how it is that all of our kids are such close friends. They want to know what we did to encourage this outcome. I want to be careful here because Steve and I made lots of mistakes with our kids. But a couple of things come to mind that may have nurtured close ties within our family. One thing we did was to give our kids a voice in decisions and to listen when they expressed their feelings, even when they were angry with us. I particularly remember one note left on our bed that said, "Dear Mom and Dad, I am very, very, very, very, very, very angry with you. I love you. Good night." I remember praying, *Thanks, God, that she can express her feelings so well!*

We also apologized for the mistakes we made and encouraged our kids to apologize to each other when they hurt each other. I had a rule that if our kids couldn't get along with each other, they had to be "best friends" for twenty-four hours, which meant they couldn't play with anyone else until they could figure out how to play with each other nicely. They even had to sleep in the same room until they could work things out. (One of our daughters jokingly says she spent more time on her brother's top bunk than in her own room for a season!) I think this helped my kids learn to respect each other and to work through their conflicts.

There will always be tension in families, but you can help build close-knit families by teaching your children to praise God for each other and by teaching them to respect each other. Today, praise God for the communion and fellowship that occur within the Trinity. Praise Him that your family life can be patterned after the loving community of the Trinity and that He is able to restore any broken relationships.

Listen

Listen to "We Need Each Other" by Sanctus Real and "To Be Like You" by Hillsong Live. As you listen, praise God for each member of your family, and then surrender all your dreams to His holiness. Praise Him by faith that He can make all things new.

Pray

Holy God, I worship You. Father, Son, and Holy Spirit, I am so grateful for each of You. I praise You that within Your relationship are eternal love and communion. Thank You for designing my earthly family after the model of the Trinity.

Holy One, I long for my family to be close. Lord, I realize as a parent I play a key role in my children getting along with one another and enjoying one another. I recognize that I set the emotional tone of our home. So much of my attitude is caught. Holy Spirit, fill me with Your Spirit so that my heart is filled with love, joy, peace, patience, kindness, goodness, faithfulness, gentleness, and self control. Holy One, I realize that if these characteristics flow out of my heart, there will be less fighting in my home. Lord Jesus, I praise You that You set the example of being humble and gentle when You were on earth. Help me to follow Your example. Lord, I know as I bow before You that You will enable me to apologize when I hurt my children's feelings so that they in turn will apologize to each other when they hurt each other.

Protect me, Father, from playing favorites because I know that favoritism in a family leads to division and sibling rivalry. Thank You that as I seek You, You will show me what it looks like to cherish and love each of my children as You love me. I praise You in advance for how You will knit our hearts together as a family unit. (Eph. 6:4; Gal. 5:22–23; 1 Peter 5:5)

Journal

In your journal today, think through your children's relation-ships with each other and with you. Is there anything you are concerned about? If so, list your worries. Is there anything you can do to help improve that relationship? Spend some time praising God that He will show you how to orchestrate developing a close-knit family.

Day 29

I will give them an undivided heart
and put a new spirit in them;
I will remove from them their heart of stone
and give them a heart of flesh.
Then they will follow my decrees and be careful to keep my laws.
They will be my people,
and I will be their God.

Ezekiel 11:19–20

The Invitation

Precious parent, I came to earth to reveal grace and truth.
Worship Me as the holy God who offers grace to those who face
their sin. I have promised you that you will know the truth,
and the truth will set you free. Praise and exalt Me that I am
able to break patterns of generational sin in your family. My
Word promises that children won't be punished for the sins of

their fathers. I will hold each generation responsible for their own sin. But, dear parent, be wise! Unless the pattern of sin is broken, sin is passed down from one generation to the next. I have called you to renounce (literally, to disown) the secret and shameful ways of your family and any patterns of deception or distortion of truth. Ask Me to reveal these patterns to you. I will gladly respond and reveal the truth to you. When you disown these sinful patterns, you are worshipping and exalting Me as Lord over your life and over your family.

I am the Lord Almighty who is holy, yet gracious. As you grow deeper in your worship, I will break the bondage of sin and the patterns of sinful behavior that have been passed down from one generation to the next. You play a critical role in this process. As you renounce any generational sin in your life, you ensure that it is not passed down to your child. (John 1:17; John 8:32; Deut. 24:16; 2 Cor. 4:2)

> Then you will know the truth, and the truth
> will set you free. (John 8:32)

Generational sins are sinful patterns that are passed down from one generation to the next. As a parent, you have a position of authority to disown any sinful patterns that have the potential to be passed down to your child. In your praise time today, ask the Holy Spirit to reveal to you any patterns of generational sin that may impact your child. Intentionally disown each and every sin, and then exalt the Lord for being a holy God who is gracious and forgiving and has the power to break the bonds of sin.

(*Note to parents of adopted children:* Even though you may not know the particulars about your child's birth family, you can still praise God for His power to break any patterns of generational sin that may have been handed down to your child. Renounce specific sins, and then praise God that He is able to free your child from those patterns of behavior.)

Listen

Today in your praise time, listen to "Forever" by Kari Jobe, "We Will Run" by Gungor, and "Victor's Crown" by Darlene Zschech. As you listen, praise God that He will reveal to you any patterns of generational sin that need to be broken.

Pray

Holy, holy, holy is the Lord. I fall on my face before You; there is no one like You in all of heaven or earth. I praise You as the Lord God Almighty who is absolutely holy. As I gaze on Your holiness, I realize how sinful I am. I praise You, Lord Jesus, because You paid the ultimate price for the atonement of my sin and the sins of my and my child's ancestors. You paid it all! Thank You. Oh, Holy One, as I look at the patterns of sin that have the potential to be passed down to my child, I feel _____ (put in an adjective describing your feelings; for example, horrified, astounded, worried). *Lord, as I bow in worship before You, I now renounce the following sinful patterns:* _____

_____ (fill in every generational sin the Holy Spirit brings to mind: lying; stealing; pride or arrogance; judgmentalism; critical spirit; sarcasm; cynicism; sexual sins such as premarital sex, infidelity, sexual abuse; addictions such as pornography, drugs, alcohol, eating disorders; suicide; rage). *Lord Jesus, I praise You that Your blood cleanses us from every sin. I exalt You because You are able to keep my child from these sins. Thank You that if he falls into any sin, You are able to forgive and restore. I praise You, Lord Jesus, for*

Your grace. How I praise You that You atoned for my sin and the sins of my children. If we repent, You continuously stand ready to forgive and to break the chain of generational sin. (Isa. 6:3–5; 2 Cor. 4:2; Isa. 6:7; 1 John 1:9)

Journal

You might want to take some extra time today or in the near future to think through your family tree and your spouse's family tree. List any sinful patterns that come to mind. If your child is adopted, list any patterns of sinful behavior that you are aware of in your child presently. Then, one by one, repent and renounce those sins. When you are finished, write a prayer praising God that He breaks the powerful chains of sin and that through the blood atonement of Jesus Christ we have freedom from sin.

Day 30

He who fears the LORD has a secure fortress,
and for his children it will be a refuge.

Proverbs 14:26

The Invitation

Precious one, it's never too early to think about the legacy you
will leave your child. Your praise honors and delights My heart!
When you exalt Me, you are creating a godly legacy for your child.
As you faithfully worship Me, you are building a secure refuge
for those who come behind you. You may think your child isn't
noticing your praise, but rest assured, she is. As your child watches
you exalt Me, her heart is softened. As you consistently praise Me,
you are less likely to fall into sin and more likely to leave a godly
heritage. My beloved one, life is short. Soon you will be with Me
for all eternity. After you are gone, your child will remember your
choice to praise Me. You have no idea how I might use that in

her life and in the life of her child. My desire is for one generation to declare My goodness to the next. I bless the children of those who make praising Me and exalting Me a priority in their home. (Prov. 14:26; Ps. 147:11; Ps. 112:2)

> But you, O Lord, sit enthroned forever;
> your renown endures through all
> generations. (Ps. 102:12)

It's never too early, nor too late, to think about the type of legacy you will leave your child. A godly inheritance is worth much more than gold or riches. Today in your praise time, exalt the Lord for the legacy you are building. Worship the Lord that His love can be passed down from one generation to another. Praise Him in advance for the way He will work in your child's life and in the lives of future generations.

Listen

Listen to "Live Like That" by Sidewalk Prophets, "A Little More Time to Love" by Steven Curtis Chapman, and "Write Your Story" by Francesca Battistelli. As you worship, praise

God that though life is short, you have the potential to leave an amazing legacy for those who will follow you.

Pray

I will exalt You, my God the King! Throughout all eternity I will be praising You. Every day I want to praise and extol Your name. You have been incredibly good to me; how can I do anything other than praise You?

I praise You in advance, Lord, because one generation will tell the next about the great things You have done in their lives. I praise and exalt You because You are able to use my story to help my child worship You. Lord, help my child to give You thanks when she remembers the great things You have done in our family. Help me to be faithful in passing down the stories of faith from the previous generations so that my child will praise You for Your goodness. I exalt You, Holy One, because You alone are worthy of all my praise. Praise and glory and wisdom and thanks and honor and power and strength all belong to You! I know that some day I will worship You for all eternity. Help me to be faithful now, because I know that life on earth is, in many ways, just the dress rehearsal for heaven. (Ps. 145:1–2, 4; Ps. 107:21–22; Rev. 7:12)

Journal

Imagine your own funeral. (I know that sounds morbid, but hang with me!) How do you want others to remember you? What type of legacy do you want to leave for your child? What changes do you need to make now so that you will be remembered as being a parent of praise?

Part Three

taking it further

praising God for His qualities

When I struggle with parental worry, fear, or anxiety, it is helpful for me to praise God for His attributes. Praise strengthens my faith and changes my focus. It lifts my eyes off my worries and on to the Almighty. He in turn quiets my anxiety and calms my fears. I've listed some of His attributes below. (You may want to add to this list.) As you praise God for His qualities, make your praise as personal as possible. For example, you might pray:

Lord, I praise You that You are almighty. I praise You that nothing catches You off guard and that nothing is too difficult for You. Thank You that I don't have to worry about _____ (name your specific worry for your child). *I exalt You that You love my child even more than I do and that You are all knowing and all wise. I praise You that I can trust You to do what's best for my child.*

All knowing—John 16:30

All wise—Romans 11:33–34

Almighty—2 Corinthians 6:18

Beautiful—Psalm 27:4

Changeless—Malachi 3:6

Comforting—Isaiah 51:12

Compassionate—Psalm 145:9

Eternal—Psalm 93:2

Excellent—Psalm 8:1 (NKJV)

Faithful—Deuteronomy 32:4

Forgiving—Nehemiah 9:17

Good—1 Chronicles 16:34

Gracious—Isaiah 30:18

Great—Psalm 145:3

Holy—Isaiah 6:3

Immortal—1 Timothy 1:17

Just—Deuteronomy 32:4

Kind—Romans 11:22

Light—1 John 1:5

Loving—1 John 4:16

Majestic—Psalm 45:4

Mighty—Psalm 24:8

Near—Matthew 1:23 (*Immanuel* means "God with us")

Overcomer—John 16:33

Powerful—Psalm 29:4

Righteous—Psalm 119:137

Sovereign—Daniel 4:25

Truth—John 14:6

Understanding—Psalm 147:5

Victorious—Psalm 45:4

Wonderful—Isaiah 9:6

Zealous—Hosea 2:19–20

Pictures of God's Character

My child's fortress—Psalm 18:2

My child's hiding place—Psalm 32:7

My child's rock—Psalm 18:2

My child's refuge—Psalm 46:1

My child's shelter—Psalm 61:4

My child's strong tower—Proverbs 18:10

praising God using His names

I believe that we often underestimate the power of using the names of God and that we can take authority over fear by using the names of God. The apostle Paul wrote, "At the name of Jesus every knee should bow, in heaven and on earth" (Phil. 2:10). We worship a triune God, and I have learned to use the names for all three persons of the Godhead in my praise time. When I have wrestled with fear or discouragement as a parent, I have purposefully chosen to praise God using His different names. When I do this, two things happen. First, my own faith is strengthened. Second, Satan flees.

Here are some sample prayers that demonstrate how to use the names of God to pray for your child.

When your child (or you) is struggling with fear:

Holy One, I praise You because You are the triune God: Father, Son, and Holy Spirit. Abba Father, You know that right now anxiety and fear are pummeling my mind. I praise You that You are almighty God over _____ (name specific situation) *in my child's life. I praise You that as the Creator You are perfectly able to create solutions for this situation. Thank You that You are the Blessed Controller of all things. This is not catching You off guard; I can trust You. I claim Your name King of Kings over my fear of* _____ (name your specific fear), *and I exalt You as Lord of Lords. Thank You that every tactic of Satan must bow under the authority of Your great name.*

When your child is having nightmares:

Lord Jesus, I praise You that You are my child's Good Shepherd. I praise You that You hover over my child as he sleeps, guarding and protecting even his dreams. Prince of Peace, I claim Your peace over my child's sleep tonight. I praise You that You are the comfort, and I thank You in advance for comforting my child.

When your child is struggling with test anxiety:

Father, I praise You that You guide my child as he goes into this exam. I exalt You as Jehovah-Jireh, my child's provider. Thank

You that as his provider You will bring to my child's memory all that he studied. Thank You, Holy Spirit, that when anxiety consumes my child during the test, You will come as the Comforter. I praise You in advance for how You will use even these exams to draw my child closer to You.

God the Father

Abba—Mark 14:36

Almighty God—Genesis 17:1

Consuming Fire—Hebrews 12:28–29

Creator—Isaiah 40:28

Deliverer—Psalm 70:5

Everlasting God—Genesis 21:33 (ESV)

Father—Isaiah 64:8

Father to the Fatherless—Psalm 68:5

Fortress—Jeremiah 16:19

Fountain of Living Waters—Jeremiah 2:13 (NLT)

God My Savior—Psalm 18:46

God My Stronghold—Psalm 144:2

God of All Comfort—2 Corinthians 1:3

God of Glory—Psalm 29:3

God of My Salvation—Habakkuk 3:17–18 (NLT)

God of Peace—Hebrews 13:20–21

God Who Sees—Genesis 16:13

Guide—Psalm 48:14

Hiding Place—Psalm 32:7

Holy One—Isaiah 43:15

Husband—Jeremiah 31:31–32

I AM—Exodus 3:14

Jehovah-Jireh—("my provider")—Genesis 22:14

Judge—Psalm 75:7

King—1 Samuel 12:12

Light—Psalm 27:1

Lord Who Heals—Exodus 15:26

Majesty in Heaven—Hebrews 8:1

Most High God—Genesis 14:18–19

Redeemer—Isaiah 54:8

Refuge—Deuteronomy 33:27

Rock—1 Samuel 2:2

Shepherd—Psalm 23:1

Shield—Psalm 5:12

Strength—Exodus 15:2

God the Son—Jesus Christ

Advocate—1 John 2:1 (ESV)

Almighty God—Isaiah 9:6

Alpha and Omega—Revelation 1:8; 22:13

Author of Life—Acts 3:15

Blessed Controller of All Things—1 Timothy 6:15 (PH)

Branch—Zechariah 3:8

Bread of Life—John 6:35

Bridegroom—Luke 5:34–35

Christ, the Son of the Living God—Matthew 16:16

Cornerstone—Ephesians 2:20; 1 Peter 2:6

Counselor—Isaiah 9:6

Creator—Colossians 1:16

Deliverer—Romans 11:26

Desire of All Nations—Haggai 2:7

Eternal Life—1 John 5:20

Everlasting Father—Isaiah 9:6

Faithful Witness—Revelation 1:5

Firstborn from the Dead—Revelation 1:5

God, Forever Praised—Romans 9:5

God of Grace—1 Peter 5:10

God of Peace—1 Thessalonians 5:23

Head over Everything—Ephesians 1:22

Heir of All Things—Hebrews 1:2

High Priest—Hebrews 4:14

Holy One—Luke 4:34; Acts 3:14;
     Revelation 3:7

Horn of Salvation—Luke 1:69

I AM—Exodus 3:14

Image of God—2 Corinthians 4:4

Immanuel—Isaiah 7:14; Matthew 1:23

Jesus—Matthew 1:21; 1 Thessalonians 1:10

King of Israel—John 1:49

King of Kings—1 Timothy 6:15

Lamb of God—John 1:29, 36

Life—John 14:6

Light of the World—John 8:12

Lion of Judah—Revelation 5:5

Living Stone—1 Peter 2:4

Lord God Almighty—Revelation 15:3

Lord of All—Acts 10:36

Man of Sorrows—Isaiah 53:3

Mediator—1 Timothy 2:5; Hebrews 12:24

Messiah—John 1:41

Morning Star—2 Peter 1:19; Revelation 22:16

Nazarene—Matthew 2:23

One and Only—John 1:14, 18; 3:16

Passover Lamb—1 Corinthians 5:7

Physician—Luke 4:23

Priest—Hebrews 5:6

Prince of Peace—Isaiah 9:6

Redeemer—Job 19:25; Isaiah 59:20

Righteous One—1 John 2:1

Rising Sun—Luke 1:78

Savior—Luke 2:11

Son of God—Matthew 27:54

Truth—John 14:6

Vine—John 15:1

Way—John 14:6

Word of God—John 1:1

God the Holy Spirit

Breath of God—Job 33:4

Comforter—John 14:16, 26 (KJV)

Counselor—John 14:16, 26

Eternal Spirit—Hebrews 9:14

Holy Ghost—Acts 20:28 (KJV)

Holy One—1 John 2:20

Holy Spirit of God—Ephesians 4:29–30

Power of the Most High—Luke 1:35

Spirit of Adoption—Romans 8:15 (ESV)

Spirit of Christ—Romans 8:9

Spirit of Faith—2 Corinthians 4:13

Spirit of God—Matthew 3:16–17

Spirit of Life—Romans 8:2

Spirit of Truth—John 14:16–17

using Scripture to praise God for His work in your child's life

I have often used a particular promise or truth to praise God in advance for His work in my child's life. When I tell parents this, I'm often asked: Is it okay to claim a verse for my child if it contains a promise given to a specific person or group of people in the Bible or a theological truth I don't completely understand? Here is my opinion on that. We don't have to understand every promise of God in order to claim it over our children. I believe we claim a promise or truth for our child and then we must bow our will to God's and trust Him with the outcome.

Here is a prayer of praise I often used, claiming Ephesians 1:3–5 for a particular child:

Praise be to the God and Father of our Lord Jesus Christ, who has blessed _____ in the heavenly realms with every spiritual blessing in Christ. For You chose _____ before the creation of the world to be holy and blameless. I praise You, Father, that You chose _____ before the creation of the world, to be adopted as Your beloved child through Jesus Christ. (Eph. 1:3–5)

I praised God by faith, even though I didn't understand the theology behind the promise. I simply chose to praise God by faith that He has chosen each of my children to be His children. God honors faith, and He honored the simplicity of my faith. When you claim a promise for your child, the important thing is that you choose to trust God, even if it looks as though He is not answering.

Here are other prayers of praise based on passages from the book of Ephesians. (Insert your child's name in the blanks.)

Lord, I praise You that You will give _____ the Spirit of wisdom and revelation so that the eyes of his heart would be opened to know the hope to which You have called him. Thank You that Your incomparable power is available to _____ as he trusts in You. That power is the same power that resurrected Christ Jesus from the dead. I praise You, Lord Jesus, that You are now seated at the right hand of the Father and that You have all power and authority over every realm and that You now hold the title that is above every other title that can be given both now and for all eternity. I exalt You, Lord Jesus, that Satan, the enemy of my child's soul, is now under Your feet. He has no authority in my child's life because of Your death and resurrection. (Eph. 1:17–22)

Lord, I worship You because though _____ was dead in her sins, You have made her alive in You. How I praise You, that You love _____ beyond what I can imagine and that You have saved her through Your grace. I praise You that _____ is Your beautiful piece of artwork created by You to do good works that You ordained in advance for her to do. How I praise You, that You will use her life for Your glory. (Eph. 2:1–4, 10)

Lord Jesus, I bow before You and adore You because through Your blood, _____ now has access to the Father. Thank You that You are a perfect mediator between my child and the Father. Thank You that _____ can approach Your throne with freedom and confidence. (Eph. 2:18)

I kneel before You, Holy One. I worship and adore You. I praise You that You will strengthen _____ with power through Your Spirit so that Christ may dwell in his heart through faith. I praise You that _____ can be rooted and established in the love You have for him. And I praise You that You will open his heart so that he will know beyond a shadow of a doubt how high and deep and wide and long is the love of Christ for him. I praise You, Almighty One, that You are able to do exceedingly abundantly beyond all _____ can ask or imagine according to Your great power. All glory, honor, and praise belong to You, Lord Jesus! (Eph. 3:14–20)

Holy Spirit, thank You that You will empower _____ to live a life worthy of her calling. I praise You that she no longer has to be infantile in her faith, blown around by every new wave of theology. I praise You that You are able to grant her the wisdom to become mature in You and strong in her faith. (Eph. 4:1–2, 14–15)

Lord Jesus, I praise You that _____ doesn't have to get drunk with alcohol but that he can be filled with Your Holy Spirit. I praise You that when my child is filled with Your Spirit, his heart will be filled with songs of joy and he will readily give You thanks and praise. (Eph. 5:18–19)

Lord Jesus, I praise You that I can clothe _____ with the armor of God every day. I praise You for the belt of truth that You offer _____. I praise You for the breastplate of Your righteousness that can protect my child's heart. Thank You for the shield of faith. Lord, I claim the shield of faith over _____'s doubts. Thank You that as she wrestles to make her faith her own, You will place the shield of Your faithfulness over her heart. Holy One, I claim the helmet of salvation over my child. I praise You that You offer salvation through Your Son, Jesus Christ. Lord, I bow before You and praise You for the gift of Your salvation and ask that at a young age _____ would receive Your salvation. Holy One, I praise You for the sword of Your Spirit, Your Word. I lift Your Word over my child. I praise You that I am always able to pray Scripture on my child's behalf and that You honor that. (Eph. 6:10–17)

You can use the prayers above as models for how to turn other scriptural promises and truths into prayers of praise. For example, "My Presence will go with you, and I will give you rest" (Exod. 33:14) can become the following prayer of praise:

Lord, I praise You that Your presence is always with _____. You go before, behind, above, and beneath my child. Thank You that knowing this gives my mind peace and rest.

Here are some of my favorite verses to claim on behalf of my children:

> Exodus 34:6–7—"The LORD, the LORD, the compassionate and gracious God, slow to anger, abounding in love and faithfulness, maintaining love to thousands, and forgiving wickedness, rebellion and sin."

> Deuteronomy 3:22—"Do not be afraid of them; the LORD your God himself will fight for you."

> Deuteronomy 4:29—"If … you seek the LORD your God, you will find him if you look for him with all your heart and with all your soul."

> Joshua 1:9—"Be strong and courageous. Do not be terrified; do not be discouraged, for the LORD your God will be with you wherever you go."

1 Samuel 26:23—"The LORD rewards every man for his righteousness and faithfulness."

2 Chronicles 15:7—"Be strong and do not give up, for your work will be rewarded."

2 Chronicles 20:15—"Do not be afraid or discouraged because of this vast army. For the battle is not yours, but God's."

Psalm 32:8—"I will instruct you and teach you in the way you should go; I will counsel you and watch over you."

Psalm 37:4—"Delight yourself in the LORD and he will give you the desires of your heart."

Psalm 84:11–12—"The LORD bestows favor and honor; no good thing does he withhold from those whose walk is blameless. O LORD Almighty, blessed is the [one] who trusts in you."

Psalm 121:8—"The LORD will watch over your coming and going both now and forevermore."

Proverbs 3:5–6—"Trust in the LORD with all your heart and lean not on your own understanding; in all your ways acknowledge him, and he will make your paths straight."

Proverbs 18:10—"The name of the LORD is a strong tower; the righteous run to it and are safe."

Isaiah 26:3—"You will keep in perfect peace him whose mind is steadfast, because he trusts in you."

Isaiah 30:18—"Yet the LORD longs to be gracious to you; he rises to show you compassion. For the LORD is a God of justice."

Isaiah 40:31—"Those who hope in the LORD will renew their strength. They will soar on wings like eagles; they will run and not grow weary, they will walk and not be faint."

Isaiah 41:10—"Do not fear, for I am with you; do not be dismayed, for I am your God. I will strengthen you and help you; I will uphold you with my righteous right hand."

Jeremiah 1:5—"Before I formed you in the womb I knew you, before you were born I set you apart."

Jeremiah 24:6–7—"My eyes will watch over them for their good, and I will bring them back to this land. I will build them up and not tear them down; I will plant them and not uproot them. I will give them a heart to know me, that I am the LORD. They will be my people, and I will be their God, for they will return to me with all their heart."

Jeremiah 29:11–13—"'I know the plans I have for you,' declares the LORD, 'plans to prosper you and not to harm you, plans to give you hope and a future. Then you will call upon me and come and pray to me, and I will listen to you. You will seek me and find me when you seek me with all your heart.'"

Lamentations 3:21–23—"Yet this I call to mind and therefore I have hope: Because of the LORD's great love we are not consumed, for his compassions never fail. They are new every morning; great is your faithfulness."

Ezekiel 11:19–20—"I will give them an undivided heart and put a new spirit in them; I will remove from them their heart of stone and give them a heart of flesh. Then they will follow my decrees and be careful to keep my laws. They will be my people, and I will be their God."

Ezekiel 34:16—"I will search for the lost and bring back the strays. I will bind up the injured and strengthen the weak."

Daniel 2:20–22—"Praise be to the name of God for ever and ever; wisdom and power are his. He changes times and seasons; he sets up kings and deposes them. He gives wisdom to the wise and knowledge to the discerning. He reveals deep and hidden things; he knows what lies in darkness, and light dwells with him."

Joel 2:25–26—"I will repay you for the years the locusts have eaten…. You will have plenty to eat, until you are full, and you will praise the name of the LORD your God, who has worked wonders for you; never again will my people be shamed."

Zechariah 4:6—"'Not by might nor by power, but by my Spirit,' says the LORD Almighty."

Matthew 6:33—"But seek first his kingdom and his righteousness, and all these things will be given to you as well."

Matthew 11:28–29—"Come to me, all you who are weary and burdened, and I will give you rest. Take my yoke upon you and learn from me, for I am gentle and humble in heart, and you will find rest for your souls."

Mark 9:23—"Everything is possible for him who believes."

Mark 11:24—"Therefore I tell you, whatever you ask for in prayer, believe that you have received it, and it will be yours."

Luke 19:10—"For the Son of Man came to seek and to save what was lost."

John 1:12—"Yet to all who received him, to those who believed in his name, he gave the right to become children of God."

John 11:25–26—"I am the resurrection and the life. He who believes in me will live, even though he dies; and whoever lives and believes in me will never die."

John 15:5—"If a man remains in me and I in him, he will bear much fruit; apart from me you can do nothing."

John 15:16—"You did not choose me, but I chose you and appointed you to go and bear fruit—fruit that will last. Then the Father will give you whatever you ask in my name."

Acts 1:8—"But you will receive power when the Holy Spirit comes on you; and you will be my witnesses in Jerusalem, and in all Judea and Samaria, and to the ends of the earth."

Romans 8:28—"And we know that in all things God works for the good of those who love him, who have been called according to his purpose."

Romans 8:38–39—"For I am convinced that neither death nor life, neither angels nor demons, neither the present nor the future, nor any powers, neither height nor depth, nor anything else in all creation, will be able to separate us from the love of God that is in Christ Jesus our Lord."

1 Corinthians 15:57—"But thanks be to God! He gives us the victory through our Lord Jesus Christ."

2 Corinthians 1:3–4—"Praise be to the God and Father of our Lord Jesus Christ, the Father of compassion and the God of all comfort, who comforts us in all our troubles, so that we can comfort those in any trouble with the comfort we ourselves have received from God."

Philippians 1:6—"Being confident of this, that he who began a good work in you will carry it on to completion until the day of Christ Jesus."

Philippians 4:13—"I can do everything through him who gives me strength."

Philippians 4:19—"And my God will meet all your needs according to his glorious riches in Christ Jesus."

Hebrews 4:16—"Let us then approach the throne of grace with confidence, so that we may receive mercy and find grace to help us in our time of need."

James 1:5—"If any of you lacks wisdom, he should ask God, who gives generously to all without finding fault, and it will be given to him."

James 4:8—"Come near to God and he will come near to you."

1 Peter 1:3–4—"Praise be to the God and Father of our Lord Jesus Christ! In his great mercy he has given us new birth into a living hope through the resurrection of Jesus Christ from the dead, and into an inheritance that can never perish, spoil or fade."

2 Peter 1:3–4—"His divine power has given us everything we need for life and godliness through our knowledge of him who called us by his own glory and goodness. Through

these he has given us his very great and precious promises, so that through them you may participate in the divine nature and escape the corruption in the world caused by evil desires."

1 John 1:9—"If we confess our sins, he is faithful and just and will forgive us our sins and purify us from all unrighteousness."

Revelation 21:4—"He will wipe every tear from their eyes. There will be no more death or mourning or crying or pain, for the old order of things has passed away."

praising God when you are grieving the death of a child

I have prayed much about what to say to parents who are in deep grief over the death of a child. Though people close to me have lost children through death or miscarriage, I have never had that experience. If you have, I want you to know I have been praying for you as I write this, and I am so sorry for your loss. I cannot begin to imagine the devastating pain you have felt—but there is One who can. God the Father watched in sorrow as His only Son, Jesus, was crucified on the cross. He promises that some day He will wipe away every tear and that there will be no more suffering and no more sorrow (Rev. 21:4). He also promises that He Himself will comfort us when we are grieving (2 Cor. 1:3–4).

Sometimes our deepest worship is our weeping. As our tears flow, we surrender all our broken dreams at the feet of the Holy One. When we worship and exalt Holy God, though we don't understand His ways, He envelops us with His love and compassion.

I asked some grieving parents what suggestions they might have for those who are mourning the loss of a child. Here is what they said:

> **1. Allow yourself to vent your anger and sorrow to God.** Don't beat yourself up or wallow in guilt for having and expressing these feelings. Jesus blessed those who honestly mourned (Luke 6:21). One way to vent your feelings is through the practice of journaling. In a journal you can write out your prayers and privately express your sorrow to God without fear of judgment from others.
>
> **2. Hang with supportive friends.** Supportive friends will *not* try to minimize or diminish your pain. They will simply

express their sorrow over your loss. They won't give you easy answers. Instead, they will feel the pain and cry with you. You need friends who, like Jesus with Martha and Mary when their brother died, will crawl into your suffering with you and weep just as so (John 11:35).

3. Consider taking a special step to remember your precious child. Some parents have purchased a piece of jewelry and had it engraved with the name of the tiny one they lost. This allowed them to remember their precious child. Others have had artwork created in remembrance or planted a tree as a memorial.

The following scriptures and songs may be helpful to use in your worship when you are grieving:

Psalm 34:18—"The LORD is close to the brokenhearted and saves those who are crushed in spirit."

Lamentations 3:21–24—"Yet this I call to mind and therefore I have hope: Because of the LORD's great love we are not consumed, for his compassions never fail. They are new every morning; great is your faithfulness. I say to myself, 'The LORD is my portion; therefore I will wait for him.'"

Isaiah 45:3—"I will give you the treasures of darkness, riches stored in secret places, so that you may know that I am the LORD, the God of Israel, who summons you by name."

Psalm 147:3—"He heals the brokenhearted and binds up their wounds."

Songs to encourage your heart:
"Held" by Natalie Grant
"God Is God" by Steven Curtis Chapman
"Sovereign" by Chris Tomlin
"Beautiful Things" by Gungor

praising God when you and your spouse disagree over parenting issues

There will likely be moments in your parenting journey when you and your spouse disagree. Praising God together often helps a couple unify. It's definitely easier to compromise when both people are on their knees and focused on praising God. However, there may be times when your spouse is not willing to praise God with you or to compromise. Here are some prayers of praise for specific situations.

If your spouse is not a believer:

Lord Jesus, I exalt You. I praise You that You are Lord over my life. Even though my spouse is not on the same page as I am spiritually, I praise You that You are able to protect my child spiritually. I praise You that You will give me wisdom moment by moment so that I can lead my child toward faith in You. Thank You that You are able to do exceedingly abundantly above all I can ask or think in my child's faith journey. I praise You that You are able to open my spouse's eyes to see how great You are. Thank You that even as my spouse watches Your work in our child's life, my spouse may be drawn to faith. Holy One, I bow before You and worship You. I ask that You would fill me, Holy Spirit, so that my spouse might see Your love in me. I praise You in advance for how You will work in my spouse's heart. (1 Cor. 7:14; Eph. 3:20; 1 Cor. 13:1)

If your spouse does not feel the need for church:

Lord Jesus, I praise You that You designed us for community. Your Word teaches that we should not give up meeting together for worship so that we can continue to grow and be encouraged in our faith. Holy One, help me to be faithful in taking my child to church, even when my spouse has no desire. You know the battle I face every weekend as I try to take my child to church. Holy One, help me to have wisdom when my spouse prioritizes sports and other activities over church attendance. I praise You that as I wait and faithfully worship You, You will show me when to stand firm and when to compromise in this area. Thank You that I don't have to worry *about changing my spouse's heart. I can leave that to You.* (Heb. 10:25; Ps. 130:5)

When you and your spouse disagree over discipline issues:

Holy One, I praise You that there are differences between my spouse and me, because this encourages us to seek You together for solutions. Lord, Your desire is that we discipline our children with love and compassion. Honestly, God, there are so many confusing theories out there on discipline. But when Jesus was here on earth, He was consistently gentle with discipline. You encourage us not to exasperate our children with harsh discipline. Teach us both to discipline creatively, gently, and always with the goal of helping our child become more like You. I praise You, Holy Spirit, that as we seek You together, You will give us both wisdom. If we err, please help us to err on the side of gentleness. (Mark 10:14–16; Eph. 6:4)

When you and your spouse disagree over the number of activities your child should be involved in:

Holy One, we live in a society that offers endless possibilities to our child in the realms of sports, music, art, and theater activities. Holy One, all of these activities cost money and time. Father, I praise You that as _____ (name your spouse)

205

and I seek You together and ask You for wisdom, You promise to answer and give us the wisdom we are asking for. Thank You that You are able to give us deeper understanding and unity about what we can afford both money wise and time wise. (James 1:5; Prov. 24:3–4)

When you and your spouse disagree over education and the best option for schooling (for example, public school, Christian school, charter school, or home school):

Lord, I praise You that You care about our child's education and that Your Word teaches us to apply our hearts to instruction and our ears to words of knowledge. Father, I praise You that there are so many options today in the realm of education. I admit that I often feel pressured by my friends to educate using the methods they are using. How I praise You that each child and family are different and that there is no one "right" way. Lord, You know that _____ (spouse's name) and I are on different pages. Holy One, I surrender my desires to Your lordship. I praise You that as I bow before You, You will open my eyes to see things from my spouse's perspective. Thank You that no matter which option we land on, You promise to use that choice for our child's benefit. (Prov. 23:12; Rom. 8:28)

lifting a mantle of praise over kids whose parents are in ministry

When we cover something with a tarp, it protects what is under it from inclement weather and overexposure to the sun. When we "lift a mantle of praise" over our kids, we are doing something similar. We are raising a protective covering over them, spiritually speaking.

I believe that Satan targets people in ministry and their children. Why? Because if he can get to our kids, he can discourage us and distract us from doing the work God has called us to do. Many nights I worried, would our kids grow up to resent church or, worse yet, the Lord?

We went through a difficult season of criticism in one church that Steve pastored, and during that time one of our kids told us, "I love Jesus, but I can't stand His church!" That night I tearfully begged God, *Please, Holy One, guard my precious child's heart. Show her that people in churches are flawed and broken, sometimes even mean, but You are good and You call us to love.* The Lord began to show me that I had to raise a mantle of praise over that child, praising Him in advance for how He would use the difficult circumstances we were facing for His glory and her good. I began to praise God that she could trust Him because He was indeed good, even when people were not so good. Many times early in the morning, on my knees, I would praise my way through different passages of Scripture for my precious teen. God honored those prayers. That teen is now married and serving in ministry in a local church!

If you are in ministry, here are some prayers for lifting a mantle of praise over yourself and your children:

Father, I praise You for the privilege of serving the church. Ministry is demanding at times, and I'm tempted to complain about how difficult it can be. Help me to remember that my children are listening. Thank You for Your promise that those who guard their mouths and their tongues keep themselves and perhaps even their family from calamity. Oh, Lord, I am aware that my children will adopt my attitude toward the church and Your kingdom. Keep me from cynicism. Jesus, I praise You because You loved children and always invited them to come to You. Help me to model Your heart for my children. (Prov. 21:23; Matt. 19:14)

Holy One, I bow before You and worship You as the only One worthy of all my praise. Help me to never fall into the pattern of worshipping success in ministry or into the pattern of finding my identity in serving You. God, so many idolize success and as a result lose their kids because they don't have enough time for both. Lord, I surrender every dream I have for successful ministry. Forgive me for the times I have been tempted to sacrifice my children on the altar of success. Holy One, protect my children. Help them to know beyond a shadow of a doubt that I treasure them. Lord Jesus, I praise You that when You ran Your earthly ministry, You weren't caught up in a showy success; instead, You came to serve. I praise You, Lord, that as I model servanthood, my child will more likely follow and serve others as well. (Mark 10:45)

God, I praise You for the opportunities You will give my child to love people who are not necessarily like him. Father, I praise You that, as my child is exposed to different cultures,

You will give him Your heart for the world. How I praise You that You came to seek and save the lost. Thank You that when my child is exposed to people who are broken or hurting, it will not contaminate him but will condition his heart toward compassion. I praise You that my child will be able to see firsthand the consequences of sin in the lives of people. Jesus, how I praise You that You prayed, "Father, protect them by the power of your name." Thank You that You will continue to intercede on my child's behalf. (Luke 19:10; John 17:11)

Abba, I bow before You and praise You because You are able to do exceedingly abundantly beyond all that I can ask or think in my child's life. I praise You that You will surround my child with Your love. Help him to be so rooted and grounded in Your love that when the criticism comes, it won't harden his heart. Open his heart to grasp how wide and deep and high is Your love for him. To You and You alone be all the glory! (Eph. 3:14–21)

God, I praise You for Your amazing creativity. Thank You that as I look to You, You will pour creativity into me, showing me how to make Sundays fun for my kids.* Thank You, Lord, that just as You created the heavens and stretched out the skies in creativity, You will pour creativity into me. Thank You that You *will take hold of my hand and show me exactly what it looks like to open my children's eyes to how fun ministry can be when we work together as a family.* (Isa. 42:5–7)

*For example: Steve used to take our kids for candy every Sunday when they survived two and sometimes three services. To this day he keeps lollipops in his church office for our staff kids.

lifting a mantle of praise over your adopted child

Adoption is near and dear to the heart of God. He adopted us into His family to be His sons and daughters. Just as earthly adoptions are risky and costly, our adoption into God's forever family cost Him the life of His own Son. What staggering love!

I have watched many couples, including my own daughter and her husband, walk the adoption journey, and I just want to say, these couples are my heroes! Even though the journey can be rough, these folks take seriously Christ's command to love and embrace the orphan. One of the greatest gifts you can give your adopted child is to lift a mantle of praise over your child.

Here are some prayers that lift a mantle of praise over your child. (Insert your child's name in the blanks.)

As you wait for your child to be born or to become a part of your family:

God, You created _____'s inmost being; you knit him together in his mother's womb. I praise You because my child is fearfully and wonderfully made; Your works are wonderful, and I know that full well. (Ps. 139:13–14)

O Lord, You are my God; I will exalt You and praise Your name, for in perfect faithfulness You have created _____. I praise You that You will do marvelous things in _____'s life—things that You planned long ago. (Isa. 25:1)

Lord, as I wait for the adoption to become final, I look to You and remind myself that You are good. Thank You that You have not given me a spirit of fear but a spirit of power, of love, and of a sound mind. I thank and praise You that You are able to quiet any anxiety and fear lurking in my heart as I set my thoughts on You. (2 Tim. 1:7 NLV; Phil. 4:6)

To break generational patterns of sin in your adopted child's family history:

I worship You, Lord, as the grace giver. I praise You that in the lineage of Your Son, Jesus Christ, there were prostitutes, thieves, liars, and murderers. When I read through the genealogy of Jesus, my heart realizes once again that Jesus came to break the power of sinful patterns and to set the captives free. I exalt You, Lord Jesus, as the One who brings freedom, and I praise You for the freedom that You speak over _____'s life. (Matt. 1:2–17; Isa. 61:1–3)

Holy One, I renounce any secret and shameful patterns, any patterns of deception or lying, any cult theology or satanist practices, any addictive behavior, sexual immorality, or any other sinful behavior that may impact _____. I praise You that You are aware of any early childhood trauma my child has experienced, any injury while still in the womb, any exposure to cultlike activity. Thank You that You are more than able to protect _____ from any dark influences. I praise You, Lord Jesus, for Your blood, and I claim the power of Your blood over my child's mind, body, and spirit. I exalt You as Lord over our home and family life. I praise You that Your blood cleanses us from all unrighteousness. I praise You that as my child bows before You and repents of any known sin, You will empower her to walk in freedom. (2 Cor. 4:1–2; 1 John 1:9)

When your adopted child struggles with feelings of insecurity and abandonment:

Lord Jesus, I praise You for my precious child. Thank You that before the foundation of the world You chose me as his parent. Holy One, I praise You that this child is loved beyond what he can imagine. I praise You that he can be rooted and grounded in my love as well as Your love. In the moments when he feels abandoned or insecure, pour Your love into his heart, whisper Your love messages into his ears, and open his eyes to the depth of Your love for him. I exalt You, Lord Jesus, because You lavish Your love on my child and You promise that You will never leave or forsake him. You are with him continuously. I praise You that You surround my child with Your loving-kindness and that Your faithfulness will never falter. (Eph. 3:17; 1 John 3:1; Heb. 13:5)

lifting a mantle of praise over children of divorce

Divorce is difficult, not only for the parent, but also for the children. If that's your story, please know I am praying for you.

Here are some sample prayers that lift a mantle of praise over a child of divorce. (Insert your child's name in the blanks.)

When your child feels rejected by your spouse, you might pray:

Lord Jesus, I praise You that You love _____ with perfect and eternal love. You continuously lavish Your love on him. Show me what it looks like to remind him daily of how much You love him. (1 John 3:1)

When you as a single parent feel fearful, you might pray:

Abba, I praise You that I don't have to feel fearful because You are continuously with me to guide and counsel me as I raise _____. I praise You that You have called me Your child and have adopted me into Your family. I praise You for Your Holy Spirit, who is ever present with me, guiding me and giving me wisdom as I seek to parent. Thank You that Your Spirit is interceding for me constantly. What a gift, Lord Jesus! In the moments when I have no idea what to do or when I feel incredibly lonely, help me to remember that Your Spirit is there to guide me. (Rom. 8:15, 26)

When you are tempted to bash your former spouse:

Lord Jesus, thank You for inviting me to be a peacemaker. Holy One, I praise You that when I am tempted to bash my former spouse, You invite me to pray for and bless him. Thank You that as I do this, my children are given a tangible example of how to forgive those who hurt them. O Lord, I know that if I continually criticize my former spouse, my children will become tense, feeling torn between us. Father, I also know that bitterness is so easily caught. Oh, Holy One, I long for my children to be free from bitterness. Thank You that I can play a part in that by modeling forgiveness and graciousness in my home. Thank You that as I faithfully praise You and keep my eyes on You, Your Spirit will empower me to do the impossible—to forgive, bless, and pray for my former spouse and that, as a result, my children will be blessed. (Matt. 5:9; Matt. 5:43–44; Matt. 5:12)

When you share custody and your former spouse is not walking with the Lord:

Lord Jesus, how I praise You that You promise that You will never, ever leave my child. He is never out of Your sight! You faithfully command legions of angels to guard my child because You love him and he is precious to You. You faithfully go with him when he spends time with my former spouse. Thank You that I can trust You to protect _____'s body, soul, and spirit. Thank You that if he feels lonely or afraid, he can cry out to You any time and You will answer him. I praise You that _____ can be strong and courageous no matter what difficulty he faces. (Heb. 13:5; Ps. 91:4–5; Isa. 43:4; Josh. 1:9)

topical index

Day 17—Fear in your child's life (teaching your child to be
        courageous)

Day 18—Chains of addiction in your child's life

Day 19—Doubt in your child's life

Day 20—Holy Spirit in your child's life

Day 21—Your child's friends

Day 22—Loss and disappointment in your child's life

Day 23—Your child's calling and purpose

Day 24—Your child's longings

Day 25—Your child's need to forgive and not judge

Day 26—Your child's need for wisdom in choosing a spouse

Day 27—Healing for your child

Day 28—Maintaining close family relationships

Day 29—Breaking the chains of generational sin

Day 30—Leaving a godly legacy

list of praise songs to download

Please note, the songs are listed in the order in which they appear in the book. This way you can download all the songs at once and develop a master playlist for your praise times.

Day	Song Title	Performed By
1	"Open Up Our Eyes"	Elevation Worship
1	"Ascribe"	New Life Worship ft. Cory Asbury
1	"Remind Me Who I Am"	Jason Gray
2	"Steady My Heart"	Kari Jobe
2	"I Will Look Up"	Elevation Worship
2	"Lord, I Need You"	Chris Tomlin
3	"We Won't Be Shaken"	Building 429
3	"Oceans"	Hillsong United
3	"You Make Me Brave"	Bethel Music and Amanda Cook
4	"Come to Me"	Bethel Music ft. Jenn Johnson
4	"You Are My Vision"	Rend Collective Experiment
4	"Help Me Find It"	Sidewalk Prophets
5	"Your Grace Finds Me"	Matt Redman

Day	Song Title	Performed By
5	"This Is Amazing Grace"	Phil Wickham
5	"Hello, My Name Is"	Matthew West
6	"The Lord Our God"	Kristian Stanfill
6	"I Wait for the Lord"	Jeremy Camp
6	"Waiting Here for You"	Christy Nockels
7	"Unfailing Love"	Chris Tomlin
7	"Your Love Is Like a River"	Third Day
7	"One Thing Remains"	Kristian Stanfill
8	"You're Not Alone"	Meredith Andrews
8	"Not Alone"	Jamie Grace
8	"He Is with Us"	Love and the Outcome
9	"Blessings"	Laura Story
9	"Overcomer"	Mandisa
10	"Worn"	Tenth Avenue North
10	"Come to Me"	Jamie Grace
10	"Psalm 62"	Aaron Keyes
11	"Everything That's Beautiful"	Chris Tomlin
11	"The Proof of Your Love"	For King & Country
12	"One Hundred Three"	Antioch Live ft. James Mark Gulley
12	"How Deep the Father's Love for Us"	Phillips, Craig and Dean
12	"Everlasting Father"	Elevation Worship
13	"Happy Day"	Tim Hughes
13	"Shake"	MercyMe
13	"God's Great Dance Floor"	Chris Tomlin

Day	Song Title	Performed By
14	"God and King"	Antioch Live ft. Stephen Gulley
14	"You Crown the Year (Psalm 65:11)"	Hillsong Live
15	"Glorious Ruins"	Hillsong
15	"It's Not Over"	Israel & New Breed
15	"You Won't Relent"	Misty Edwards
16	"The First and the Last"	Hillsong Live
16	"Be Still"	Bethel Music and Steffany Frizzell Gretzinger
17	"Revelation Song"	Kari Jobe
17	"Great I Am"	Jared Anderson
17	"Christ Is Risen"	Matt Maher
18	"God Who Saves"	Antioch Live
18	"Where the Spirit of the Lord Is"	Hillsong Live
18	"Hurricane"	Natalie Grant
19	"Give Me Faith"	Elevation Worship
19	"King of Heaven"	Paul Baloche
19	"Holding On"	Jamie Grace
20	"Fall Afresh"	Bethel Music and Jeremy Riddle
20	"Spirit Speaks"	All Sons & Daughters
20	"Breathe On Us"	Kari Jobe
21	"Friend of God"	Phillips, Craig and Dean
21	"Love Goes On"	Hillsong Young & Free
21	"Show Jesus"	Jamie Grace
22	"Need You Now (How Many Times)"	Plumb
22	"Cornerstone"	Hillsong Live

Day	Song Title	Performed By
22	"Anchor"	Hillsong Live
23	"My God"	Desperation Band
23	"My Hope"	Paul Baloche
23	"Born for This (Esther)"	Mandisa
24	"Come to the Water"	Kristian Stanfill
24	"My Soul Longs for You"	Misty Edwards
25	"Search My Heart"	Hillsong United
25	"Come Thou Fount of Every Blessing"	Sara Groves
26	"Oh How I Need You"	All Sons & Daughters
26	"You Never Fail"	Hillsong Live
27	"I Surrender"	Hillsong Live
27	"Even If (The Healing Doesn't Come)"	Kutless
28	"We Need Each Other"	Sanctus Real
28	"To Be Like You"	Hillsong Live
29	"Forever"	Kari Jobe
29	"We Will Run"	Gungor
29	"Victor's Crown"	Darlene Zschech
30	"Live Like That"	Sidewalk Prophets
30	"A Little More Time to Love"	Steven Curtis Chapman
30	"Write Your Story"	Francesca Battistelli

acknowledgments

Special thanks to:

My husband, Steve. Babe, we survived parenting together. There is no one on the face of this earth that I would rather have parented our four kids with. You brought so much wisdom to our home. Thank you for going the extra mile with each of our kids and for modeling Jesus to them. I praise God for you.

My kids:

Bethany, wow! I could never thank you enough for all your work on this book. The wisdom and editing you brought were incredibly valuable. Thank you for orchestrating the field test and for communicating with those around the country who field-tested the principles in this book. I have such great memories of you as a child. One of my favorites is when you petitioned our children's ministries director for more gym time for the girls coming to Wednesday night programs. You were only in third grade, but your petition was so compelling you won. You were communicating well even back then. I praise God for how you have continued to praise Him in your own parenting journey and for how you are raising your sons, Tyler and Zachary, to praise God. I love you, Bo, and praise God for you!

Josiah, I praise God for your leadership skills and your wise thoughts on fatherhood. Thank you for reviewing *The 30-Day Praise Challenge for Parents* from the perspective of a father. What a gift! You are an incredible father to Joshua. I love the way you pray over him and even film yourself praying over him for the times you have to travel. I have great memories of teaching you Joshua 1:9 and watching you strut around the house as a preschooler, chanting, "Be strong and courageous!" And now you are teaching your own son that same verse. How cool is that? I love you, JJ, and praise God for you!

Stefanie, you are an amazing and fun mom. It is so much fun to hear you have morning praise time with Charlie and Selah and listen to you teaching them Scripture verses. I have so many fun memories of you as a child. Remember how you came home from church and challenged your dad and me, asking, "Where in the Bible does it say it's a sin to dye your hair blue?" Thankfully, Dad had the wisdom to say "nowhere" and that you were welcome to dye it blue if you wanted to. I praise God for how you listen for God's Spirit and for how you speak hope to others. Thank you for the wisdom you brought to this book, Stef. I love you and praise God for you!

Kerith, I love your passion for praise and worship. From the time you were a tiny child, I remember tucking you in bed at night, praying over you, and then hearing you sing yourself to sleep as I walked down the hall. Now, it is such an incredible joy to watch and hear you lead worship. I think the angels cry from the joy of hearing you sing "Revelation Song." Never stop leading others into God's presence! Thank you for all the songs you helped me find for this book and for making praise such a priority in your life. I love you, Bearsy, and praise God for you!

My sons-in-law and daughter-in-law:

Chris, you have a heart for God and bring so much wisdom to your home. You love Bethany, Tyler, and baby Zachary with a love that reflects Christ. It's amazing watching you be a part of Ty's pretend band when he plays church and leads "Manifesto"! I love you, Chris, and praise God for you!

Shaina, you are so gentle, wise, and loving! Thank you for being a part of the field test for this book. Your insight was invaluable. You are an amazing and fun wife for JJ and an incredible mom to Joshua. I love you, Shainey, and praise God for you!

Dave, you have such a heart for Jesus and for the broken and lost. I love seeing you play guitar in the worship band at church and watching you bring Stef flowers and take Charlie and Selah on special "Daddy" dates! I love you, Dave, and praise God for you!

Zach, you are incredibly passionate about God and about people. You and Keri consistently open your home to friends. Dad and I love how your home has become a sanctuary of hope and encouragement for so many. I know the Lord has a special anointing on your life, and I love the way you show Christ to the guys on your ship. I love you, Zach, and praise God for you!

My grandkids:

Charlie, I love your passion for Jesus and those who are hurting. It's hard to believe you are four years old already. One of my favorite things is hearing you pray. You have such deep concern for the homeless and those who don't have enough food. You are so great at memorizing verses! I love you, precious Charlie, and can't wait to see how God uses you!

Tyler, I love your passion for worship and praise. Even though you are only three and a half, you enjoy nothing more than playing your drums and guitar and holding church services. It's amazing to hear you try to preach like your papa. When you sing "Manifesto" and "10,000 Reasons," Jesus smiles. I know God has a special anointing on your life. I love you, precious Ty, and can't wait to watch all that God does through your life.

Joshua, I love how your eyes light up and how you dance when the music starts at church. You're only nineteen months, yet you grab hands at the dinner table, close your eyes, and say, "Dear Jesus." Oh, you bring so much joy to Jesus's heart! I love you, Joshua, and can't wait to see how God uses you in His kingdom.

Selah, I love you, precious princess. You sparkle with your big blue eyes, and you bring joy to every room you enter. It's so much fun to hear you sing in your car seat when your mama turns on the music. Jesus shines through you, little one. You have so much personality! I love you, sweet Selah, and can't wait to see all that God does through you!

Baby Zachary, our "chosen" grandchild. I love your little sweet snuggles. Oh, precious one, you have been prayed for by hundreds. Your mommy and daddy named you Zachary, "God remembers." Precious one, may you never forget that God remembers. He will use you mightily to bring hope to others. I love you, precious Zachary, and praise God for you!

My incredible editor, Liz Heaney. This is the fifth book we've worked on together! You bring so much wisdom to each project. God has used you in remarkable ways to build my confidence as a writer. I thank God for you all the time. Thanks for understanding my heart and for helping me give voice to my thoughts. I love you and praise God for you, Liz!

Linda Dillow, I could never thank you enough for originally giving me the praise challenge. It's amazing to think of how God has multiplied that challenge and now given it to thousands. I love you and praise God for you!

To all the women who field-tested this book. You were incredible.

Ashley Holderness, thanks for all your help administrating both Steve's life and my life. What would we do without you? Thanks for all the help you gave to this project, Ashley.

Jarred and Heather Butler, I am so thankful for both of you and for all you bring to the Becky Harling Ministries. The web stuff, all the social media help you give me, and just how amazing you both are. I love you both and am so thankful for you!

Justin Bullis, my worship pastor. Thanks so much for all your help with the music for this book and for faithfully leading us into the presence of God at church.

Ingrid Beck and all the others at David C Cook publishing. It is such a privilege to be published by you. Thank you for believing in me and in the worth of this book.

If you have a question or comment
you would like to share with Becky,
she would love to hear from you.
You can connect with her on:

Facebook: www.facebook.com/
beckyharlingministries

Twitter:
www.twitter.com/BeckyHarling

Pinterest:
www.pinterest.com/beckyharling